THE FREEDOM OF THE WILL

THE
FREEDOM
OF THE
WILL

BY

J. R. LUCAS

Fellow of Merton College, Oxford

ἐπεὶ κρεῖττον ἦν τῷ περὶ θεῶν μύθῳ κατακολουθεῖν ἢ τῇ
τῶν φυσικῶν εἱμαρμένη δουλεύειν· ὁ μὲν γὰρ ἐλπίδα παραιτή-
σεως ὑπογράφει θεῶν διὰ τιμῆς, ἡ δὲ ἀπαραίτητον ἔχει τὴν
ἀνάγκην.

Epicurus, letter to Menoeceus, 134

CLARENDON PRESS · OXFORD

1970

Oxford University Press, Ely House, London W.1

GLASGOW NEW YORK TORONTO MELBOURNE WELLINGTON
CAPE TOWN SALISBURY IBADAN NAIROBI DAR ES SALAAM LUSAKA ADDIS ABABA
BOMBAY CALCUTTA MADRAS KARACHI LAHORE DACCA
KUALA LUMPUR SINGAPORE HONG KONG TOKYO

PRINTED IN GREAT BRITAIN BY
WILLIAM CLOWES AND SONS, LIMITED
LONDON AND BECCLES

To

E. de G. L.
1878–1958
and
E. de G. L.
1962–

CONTENTS

§I

FREEDOM AND PHILOSOPHY

THE three great problems of philosophy, according to Kant,[1] are God, freedom, and immortality. Of these, freedom, that is, the Freedom of the Will, is the one most accessible to reason, and has continued to perplex us to the present day. We have a profound conviction of freedom. We know we are free. Yet when we think of ourselves from a scientific point of view, we do not see how we can be free. It would be a denial of science, we feel, to make man an exception to the universal laws of nature, and say that although everything else could be explained in terms of cause and effect, men were different, and were mysteriously exempt from the sway of natural laws. Men, scientifically speaking, are no different from anything else. There is no special privilege of humanity, so far as science is concerned, which makes human behaviour not susceptible of scientific enquiry and scientific explanation. There must be causes of human behaviour, as there are causes of everything else. To think otherwise is pure superstition. For there is no evidence to the contrary, and already physiologists, neurologists, and psychologists have been remarkably successful in explaining human behaviour. To maintain a doctrine of freedom in the face of these facts is mere anthropomorphic obscurantism.

And yet we are reluctant to surrender our freedom without a struggle. The doctrine that we are not free runs counter to something we know to be true so surely that only the most irrefragable arguments could shake the intimations of our everyday experience. Moreover, if we did abandon our belief in freedom, we should have to abandon much else in our view of ourselves and of our moral and rational life. Nor is it clear that we ought not to think anthropomorphically. After all, we are men: we do regard men, ourselves and others, as being different from the rest of creation. Men are rational, and ought to be treated not merely as means,

---

[1] *Critique of Pure Reason*, A3/B7; A337n/B395n.

but always also as ends. We condemn the nazis for regarding non-Aryan men as mere animals, and treating them scientifically, as mere objects of scientific research. We are entitled at least to put the case against freedom to the test. The claim needs to be stated with precision, and the arguments expressed in full, and counter-arguments considered. Much depends on the conclusion. If it be superstition to believe in freedom, and we conclude in favour of freedom, we shall be committed to superstition.[1] If, on the other hand, we conclude that man is not free, we may have to revise many of our present concepts about man and morality, responsibility and punishment, history and humanity. Kant was right in thinking freedom to be an unavoidable problem set by pure reason, though wrong in despairing of the power of reason to solve it. For the very fact that freedom is a problem for reason is itself a reason for believing that we are free. Many men have sensed this, but the argument is extremely difficult to articulate and assess. I have attempted to articulate it in Section 21, and in the following sections to reformulate it in formal terms with the aid of a profound theorem of mathematical logic discovered by Gödel in 1929. It is a controversial argument, and I have tried to meet objections raised against it, for I believe it to be ultimately a decisive argument which will refute the one sort of determinism— physical determinism—which seriously worries men today. But it is not the only argument, and its bearing is difficult to assess except in the context of the whole debate; and in the first two thirds of the book I discuss, in a more orthodox fashion, the main points at issue, to which innumerable men have contributed many arguments in many forms. I have not tried to do justice to them. Exhaustive treatments are exhausting. Moreover, philosophy has to be self-thought if it is to be thought at all. It is an activity, rather than a set of propositions. Each man needs to think out the problems and their solutions for himself, and although other men's philosophizing may help him in his own, he cannot accept their conclusions, or even understand their arguments, until he has already argued a lot with himself. I have aimed to be, so far as one can be, unsophisticated. The footnotes are intended to supply the deficiency, and show the reader where he can follow up any particular line of argument in greater detail and with greater

[1] Compare G. J. Warnock, "Actions and Events", in D. F. Pears, ed., *Freedom and the Will*, London, 1963, p. 79.

subtlety. Although I think some conclusions can be reasonably well established, I do not offer any formal proofs, but only, I hope, show how one may think one's way through to these conclusions for oneself. But only the reader, not I, can carry the programme through.

RESPONSIBILITY AND FREEDOM

OUR concern with freedom is connected with our concept of responsibility. The word 'responsible' comes from the Latin *respondeo*, I answer. It means 'answerable', 'accountable'. If I am responsible for a particular deed, I have to answer a certain question, namely the question 'Why did you do it?', while if I am not responsible, then that question is one which cannot be addressed to me; or if it is addressed to me, I am not obliged to answer it, at least not in the terms in which it is put.

Normally we are responsible for our actions. Indeed, it is a condition of an action's being thought of as really my own that I should be open to the question 'Why did you do it?'—I "own up" to a (mis-)deed by saying 'I did it', and thereby inviting the question 'Why did you do it?', and laying myself open to blame if I cannot explain my action satisfactorily. To explain one's action is to give a satisfactory answer to the question 'Why did you do it?'. Many different sorts of answer may on occasion be accounted satisfactory: but they have, characteristically, two features: they are reasons; and they were my reasons. They are reasons, not only why I did, but why one should, act in the way I did. This is how my explanation can be an explanation. It enables my hearer to see why I acted as I did. But they are not only reasons, covertly universal and claiming to have some purchase on any reasonable man: they are *my* reasons, reasons I have chosen to act upon, reasons I have thereby made my own.

We set great store by our actions, and by being able to explain and justify them. It is only through our actions that we can achieve anything in the public external world. We therefore, normally, want to be responsible for them. We want them to be ours, and we want to be able to explain them, and subject them to rational evaluation. For only so can we achieve anything worthwhile. Therefore, normally, we want to be held responsible, and claim our actions as our own. But sometimes we do not. Sometimes we want to disown an action others ascribe to us, occasionally out of modesty, usually because the action, as described, would bring us no credit. We cannot give a satisfactory answer to the question 'Why did you do it?', and sometimes can legitimately object to the question, and say it is one which ought not to be asked of us, and which we cannot be required to answer.

The question 'Why did you do it?' may fail in different ways. It may fail on account of the *did*, or of the *you*, or of the *it*. A boy who is allowed to sail in the harbour and is rescued from the open sea, may ward off the question 'Why did you sail out to sea?' with the defence 'I did not. The wind dropped suddenly, and I was carried out by the tide.' Aristotle would describe it as ἀκούσιον (involuntary), because it had come about βίᾳ (by *force majeure*).[1] We might put it better by saying that it was not a deed, something that the boy did, but a situation or predicament, something that he was caught up in. We cannot ask him to explain his actions, because they were not his actions. The active voice was out of place in our question; not 'Why *did* you sail out to sea?' but 'Why *were* you swept out to sea?' The passive voice allows us to offer sympathy and help to the patient, but debars us from demanding explanations or imputing blame.

The question may fail also on account of the *you* or the *it*. Such cases are often of great importance to lawyers. Thus mistaken identity, where the question fails because addressed to the wrong person. 'Why did you do it?' '*I* did not do it: he did.' So, too, the many cases where the description of the action is objected to. 'Why did you kill him?' 'I did not kill him: all I did was to fire at the target, but the bullet ricocheted.' Here the person questioned is not denying that he did something, but is objecting to the questioner's word for what he did: the action, for which he does not deny responsibility, has been wrongly described, and the controversy is about the right description of what the agent did. Aristotle discusses this sort of defence under the heading δι' ἄγνοιαν (ignorance).[2] In the typical case, where a man is being blamed for having brought about some untoward event, he will disclaim responsibility by saying that he did not *know* that the untoward event would be a consequence of the action he agrees

[1] *Nicomachean Ethics* III, 1, 1110a1–4.
[2] *Nicomachean Ethics* III, 1, 1110b18–1111a20.

that he certainly did do. Often, however, he will say 'I did not mean to do it', and often he will use some other more specific word to indicate what has gone wrong. 'I did not realise', 'I was not thinking', 'It was a mistake', 'I was acting under a misapprehension.' The study of these phrases reveals subtle and important distinctions between different types of mental lapse, important to the moralist and lawyer, and interesting for the philosophy of mind.[1] But such cases pose no problem of freedom. In other cases, however, a problem of freedom does arise. We may repudiate responsibility not on the score of a straightforward mistake of identity or misdescription, but because the action imputed to us fails to be our action for other more elusive reasons. Aristotle gives as a paradigm of *force majeure* the case where our bodily movements are under the control of other people.[2] If my hand is placed on the trigger, and made to tighten by electrical stimulation of the muscles, I should reject the question 'Why did you shoot him?', and say 'I did not shoot him. I did not pull the trigger. My muscles tightened in response to electrical stimulation.' Here we are partly rejecting the *did*—it was not a deed I did but something that happened to me. We are also partly rejecting the *you*—it was not I who had a hand in it, but my body: we try to draw a distinction between "I", the real active *ego*, and "me", or "my body", or some part of my body, which is regarded more as a part of my external environment than as what I really am myself. So we say 'It was not I who kicked him, it was just my knee jerking.' 'I wanted to, but my stomach would not let me.' We are not simply saying that the word 'you' is wrongly addressed—it is not a case of mistaken identity, the right question addressed to the wrong person; we agree, by use of the word 'my' in 'my body' 'my knee' that the person addressed is the relevant person, but claim the whole use of the second person, no matter to whom addressed, is inappropriate and ought to be replaced by a verb in the third person ('it' rather than 'he') in physiological event-language rather than personal action-language. It was the wrong question—wrong part of wrong verb—addressed to the right person.

[1] See J. L. Austin: "A Plea for Excuses", *Proceedings of the Aristotelian Society*, 1956; reprinted in J. L. Austin, *Philosophical Papers*, Oxford, 1961.
[2] *Nicomachean Ethics* III, 1, 1110a1-4.

Aristotle half assimilates to these cases, where I am not in control of my body, another set of cases where I act "under duress", that is, where I am in control of my body but am not in control of the situation and do not have any real choice.[1] I disclaim responsibility for actions done at the pistol point, much as I do for bodily reactions induced by electrical stimulation. If a dictator has my family in his power, and will kill them if I do not do his bidding, I have no choice but to obey. A sailor in a storm may have to jettison his cargo to save his ship; but can hardly be said to have done it voluntarily, or of his own free will. We therefore may be tempted to say that he acted involuntarily, and for that reason is not to blame. But this is a mistake. The word 'voluntary' is not the contradictory of 'involuntary'.[2] 'Voluntary' is to be contrasted with 'paid' (work), 'conscribed' (military service), 'prudential' (acts of courtesy), or 'morally obligatory' (acts of kindness). The box at the back of a church marked 'Free-will offerings' has nothing to do with the freedom of the will about which St. Augustine wrote. The sense is of there not being a reason of some typical sort. And this is just what is not true of the sailor jettisoning his cargo. He has a reason, a very good reason. He did not voluntarily throw it overboard: but nonetheless it was not an involuntary reaction. We ought not to say that it was something for which he was not responsible. He is responsible: but, when asked the question 'Why did you do it?', he has a perfectly good answer, 'I did it in order to save the ship.' We do not blame the sailor for jettisoning the cargo; but not because it was a non-action for which he was non-answerable, but because it was a proper action for which he can give an entirely adequate account.

So too, perhaps, the man whose family is in the dictator's power. He is not to be blamed; not because he had no choice, and therefore did not really *do* what he is said to have done, but because he had overwhelming reasons for doing as he did, which excuse, even if they do not justify, his actions. We can exculpate without having to make out that a man did not really do what he did do. So too, perhaps, the man at pistol point, or the man who lets out a secret under torture. But the cases merge into those where we cannot regard the man's responses as his actions.

[1] *Nicomachean Ethics* III, 1, 1110a4–1110b17.
[2] I owe this point to the late J. L. Austin, in a seminar.

Flinches, spasms, reflexes—we cannot ask a man his reasons for doing these. They really are involuntary. And there is no clear boundary-line between those things that overstrain human nature, which no one can resist, and those that there is no excuse for giving into. Hence the temptation to assimilate them.

There are many different types of situation in which we feel that what appear to be actions are not really the actions of a person, and the advance of knowledge has increased their number. Besides the physiological conditions mentioned—reflexes, spasms, tics, automatisms—and drunkenness, which caused Aristotle some difficulty, we now would reckon some psychological conditions—kleptomania, for example—to preclude putative actions from really being actions. It is not possible to give a precise and complete list, because it is likely that further advances in psychological knowledge will add to it: nor is it at all easy to formulate exactly a general criterion; Aristotle suggests that it turns on whether the initial move, ἡ ἀρχὴ τοῦ κινεῖν τὰ ὀργανικὰ μερή, was inside or outside the agent.[1] But this is too vague to be a criterion. Moreover, the concept 'I' is an elusive one.[2] However far I have analysed my situation, I can always step back, and view it from the outside. I can distinguish not only my body from my real self, but my mind, my psychological make-up, my personality. All these can be regarded as something other than myself, which I have to take account of when I am deciding what to do, just as much as I have to take account of external circumstance. When we think about the self, it seems like an onion. We always want to peel off another skin, in order to lay the real self bare, but if we peel off all the skins there may be nothing left.[3] We begin to suspect that 'I' is not only elusive to our search, but eliminated by it. Aristotle's formula does not solve the problem of responsibility, but only re-states it in a more intractable form.

The same difficulty has been sensed in unsophisticated thought. Although they have not formulated any philosophical doctrine of the self, most people do not believe that kleptomaniacs are really responsible for their thieving. We accept that some

[1] *Nicomachean Ethics* III, 1, 1110a15–19.

[2] See also Gilbert Ryle, *The Concept of Mind*, London, 1949, Ch. VI Section 7, pp. 195–198.

[3] See also F. H. Bradley, *Appearance and Reality*, Oxford, 1955, Ch. IX, esp. pp. 77–78.

psychological conditions, as much as some bodily conditions, make people unable to do, or unable not to do, certain things, for which, therefore, we cannot properly ask their reasons. With the advance of knowledge, we have come to accept more conditions as being of this sort. And the suspicion is that with further progress more and more such conditions will be recognized, until ultimately it will emerge that there are no actions that a person can properly be said to have done, and that what hitherto had been described as actions were all really only the reactions of a complex organism responding to complicated stimuli. The Athenians applied the concept of 'responsible' widely and held inanimate objects which caused the death of men accountable and brought them to trial before the Areopagus; but with a greater understanding of the determined character of natural phenomena, they allowed the practice to fall into desuetude: in the Middle Ages, animals which were the cause of death could be haled before a court and on condemnation be made *deodand*: and until the last century kleptomaniacs were sent to prison and insane killers hanged. In each of these cases a greater understanding of natural laws and a widening of the scope over which they were believed to be applicable, was followed by a corresponding reduction in the extension of the concept 'free'. And so too now, "... as our psychological and physiological knowledge of human actions and reactions increases, the range of human actions of which we can reasonably say 'an alternative action was possible' or 'he could have acted otherwise' necessarily diminishes."[1] If the process continues to a conclusion we shall stop regarding men ever as free agents, and account for all their actions in terms of their environment and heredity and nothing else.

[1] Stuart Hampshire, *Spinoza*, Penguin, 1951, p. 151; quoted, J. B. Wilson, "Freedom and Compulsion", *Mind*, LXVII, 1958, p. 61. See also Isaiah Berlin, *Historical Inevitability*, Oxford, 1954, p. 20; reprinted in *Four Essays on Liberty*, Oxford, 1969, p. 58.

§3

THE COMMON SENSE REPLY

MANY modern philosophers are unconvinced by the suggestion that increasing knowledge may leave no room for freedom. Some offer an alternative analysis of freedom and responsibility.[1] Some argue that whatever the correct analysis of these concepts is, they cannot be shown to be always inapplicable. For after all, we do use them. We do describe some actions as free actions, and ascribe to the agents responsibility for them: and on other occasions we refuse to allow the words to be applied. We thus use the words to pick out some situations in contrast to others, and since the meaning of a word, they say, is given by its use, the meaning of these words is given by their use, and therefore it cannot be the case that they are always incorrectly used. In their use of language, all the people cannot—logically cannot—be fooled all the time. For language is constituted by their use of it.[2]

The argument is best illustrated by an analogy. An undergraduate returned home after his first term reading psychology flushed with the knowledge that all motives were at bottom sexual. His aunt was duly shocked when told that her churchgoing was merely sublimated sex, and that her cooking for the Women's Institute competition was a substitute for sex, and that her going to art exhibitions was a compensation for her lack of sex-life, and that her weekly stint for Meals-on-Wheels was really an alternative form of sex satisfaction. But after a couple of vacations she got wise to her nephew's mode of thought, and cheerfully agreed that everything was sex, and that all motives were sexual, and that all activities were manifestations of the *libido*. She had no objection to sex at all, she said; but only to sexy sex. She had no objection to the ordinary manifestations of

---

[1] See next section.

[2] See, *e.g.*, A. G. N. Flew, "Divine Omnipotence and Human Freedom", in A. G. N. Flew and A. C. MacIntyre, eds., *New Essays in Philosophical Theology*, London, 1955, pp. 149–153, and 163–164.

sex—such as church-going, talking to other women, looking at pictures, or helping old people—but only to those manifestations of sex that were concerned with the genitals. The undergraduate was at a loss for a reply. By using the word 'sex' to cover all types of human activity, he had deprived it of its normal association with the genital organs, and thus deprived it of its power to shock and distress his aunt. It is only because the word 'sex' is not applied to some sorts of human activity that it has any meaning. It obtains its meaning from being applied to some activities and relations—copulation, courtship, marriage—and not to others—scientific research, friendship, philanthropy. Remove the contrast, and you take away the meaning. It may be possible to redraw the boundaries slightly: but there must be some boundary. It may be possible to argue that some sorts of religious, social, artistic, or philanthropic activity are really sexual. But we cannot claim that they all are. There must be something excluded, or else there is nothing being said.

A similar mistake was made by the Ionian philosophers, Thales, who said that all things were made of water, and Anaximenes, who said that all things were made of air. In each case we protest: if everything is made of water, how does the word 'water' have any meaning? It is only by reserving the word 'water' for some thing and not other things that the word carries any sense. If we expand the range of application of the word to cover everything, we evacuate it of all content. With words, as with titles "If everyone is somebodee, then no one's anybody." We therefore rule out, on principle, as a matter of linguistic necessity, all sweeping claims beginning with the word 'all'. And in particular, we state, categorically, that it cannot be the case that all actions are un-free.

It is clear that this is itself a sweeping claim. It rules out, among other things, all statements of metaphysics, purporting to tell us, in general terms, what the world is really like. Although there is some force in the claim, we should be suspicious of it stated in such uncompromisingly general terms. It depends on a theory of language—that the meaning of a word is its use—interpreted in the sense that the meaning of each word is separately constituted by the range of cases in which it is correctly applied. And this is false. Many words are defined not simply ostensively, by a range of cases, but by relation to other words. Philosophers have often mistakenly assumed that all words are like colour words. Colour words are defined ostensively, and obtain their meaning from being applied to some shades and not to others. And if any one were minded to argue that, say, all things were red, he would be committing an "Ionian Fallacy", and could be refuted by the argument we have given. But most words are not like colour words. The use which determines their meaning is partly an intra-linguistic use. It is not a simple matter of applying or not applying the word in some standard case, but a complicated matter of patterns of entailment and presumption between sentences containing it and sentences containing only other words. And there is no *a priori* argument to show that we can never discover that some word is never applicable, and hence that its contradictory is always applicable. It seems that 'free' is such a word. It is not a simple, surface term whose misuse can be cured by careful linguistic analysis. We use the word 'free' not simply to characterize a certain class of actions which we could, so to speak, pick out by eye, but rather to say of those actions that no complete causal account can be given of them. Thus when it seems that a complete causal account could be given of an action, or of a class of actions, we cease to apply the word 'free' and say instead that they are determined by the laws of nature in conjunction with their antecedent circumstances. Actions which we once regarded as free we no longer do: we have redrawn the boundaries of the extensions of the concepts 'free' and 'determined' as our understanding of psychology has deepened. In so doing we have not altered the meanings of the two words, because their meanings are not given by their extension but by their intension. It is not that we have changed their meaning but that in order to preserve their meaning we have had, in the light of new knowledge, to alter their application. So, likewise, in Intuitionist mathematics, the discovery of a constructive proof of a theorem will result in our admitting that theorem as a theorem, which before we were unwilling to do. It is not that we have changed the meaning of the word 'theorem', but that the meaning goes deep, and it cannot always be determined immediately or with certainty whether a particular application of the word is correct or not. Simple-minded linguistic analysis is no more use in solving the problem of determinism than it is in dealing with problems of provability in the philosophy of mathematics.

The mathematical analogy holds in a further respect: the concept of being determined, like the concept of being a theorem acceptable to the Intuitionists, is what I shall call an " aggressive " concept. The extensions of these concepts are likely to increase at the expense of their contradictories, but not to decrease. We may discover that a particular action or class of actions is determined, or that a particular statement is a theorem, but hardly the other way. Nor is it going to be nearly so easy to establish the negative generalisation, that there is no complete causal explanation, or no constructive proof, as it is to show the particular positive fact that there is a complete causal explanation, namely this . . . ., or that there is a constructive proof, namely this . . . . . The fear is, rather, that with the advance of knowledge the concept 'determined' will continue to aggress, and the concept of 'free' to "regress" until the former covers every case, the latter none.

§4

NECESSITY AND CONSTRAINT

ALTHOUGH the general argument for always preserving the *status quo* is bound to fail, it may still be true that freedom and responsibility, when properly analysed, will be found to be immune to revision, or at least to elimination. It has been traditionally assumed that freedom is opposed to necessity, or predictability, or causal explicability. But, some philosophers have argued,[1] this is a mistake. What relieves a man of responsibility is constraint (or compulsion), not necessity. That, after all, was what Aristotle meant by τὰ βίᾳ γινόμενα. Constraint defeats responsibility because it is not at all up to the individual concerned whether the *soi-disant* action take place or not; what he decides is irrelevant; it happens willy-nilly, so far as he is concerned. It is, they allege, a complete confusion to suppose that determinism has any bearing on freedom, responsibility, or the moral life. It is only, they say, our unfortunate habit of speaking of Laws of Nature, that has led us to think of them as prescribing the future, instead of, as really, simply describing events, economically and compendiously, just as they occur, without in any way telling them how they are to happen. If only we would

[1] Hobbes, *Of Liberty and Necessity*, London, 1654; reprinted in *English Works of Thomas Hobbes*, ed. Sir William Molesworth, London, 1840, Vol. IV, pp. 229–278; *The Questions concerning Liberty, Necessity and Chance*; reprinted in *English Works*, Vol. V. Hume, *Treatise on Human Nature*, bk II, part III, Section 3. The University of California Associates, "The Freedom of the Will", in *Knowledge and Society*, New York, 1938; reprinted in Herbert Feigl and Wilfrid Sellars, eds., *Readings in Philosophical Analysis*, New York, 1949. Bertrand Russell, *Our Knowledge of the External World*, London, 1949, pp. 231–240; reprinted in "On the Notion of Cause with Application to the Free-Will Problem", in Herbert Feigl and Mary Brodbeck, eds., *Readings in the Philosophy of Science*, New York, 1953, pp. 402–407. Moritz Schlick, *Problems of Ethics*, tr. David Rynin, New York, 1939, Ch. VII, esp. Section 3, pp. 148–149. A. J. Ayer, "Freedom and Necessity", *Polemic*, **5**, 1946, reprinted in *Philosophical Essays*, London, 1954.

take Natural Laws as stating regularities rather than laying down rules, the bogey of determinism would be laid, and we should be free to enjoy the present and predict the future to our hearts' content. Let us eat, drink and be merry, nay, let us reason, deliberate and make moral decisions, and tomorrow do whatever it is that we shall do.

The claim that 'freedom' *means* absence of constraint is a difficult one to discuss. The word 'freedom' has many meanings, among them absence of constraint. A man is free in this sense, when he is not incarcerated in gaol. It is an important sense, particularly for lovers of civil liberty. But it is not the only sense. We also speak of a man being free when he is not forbidden by an identifiable person or rule from doing something; or again we speak of a man being free when he has no cause to fear that some real or apprehended evil will come to pass. In mechanics we talk about degrees of freedom; and in other sciences we talk of free energy, free radicals, free variables.[1] We cannot say of any one sense that it is *the* sense. It might be the case that absence of constraint is the relevant sense of 'freedom' when we are discussing the freedom of the will, but it needs arguing for.

One argument has been given. The relevant sense of freedom is the one connected with responsibility, and constraint defeats responsibility. But for this argument to be valid, we should have to maintain also that constraint is the only condition which defeats responsibility. In the literal sense of the word 'constraint', this is simply not true. We hold people not responsible for their actions not only when their bodies are under the physical control of other people, but in many other circumstances. A kleptomaniac is not, literally, constrained to steal—his is a different case from that of the man whose muscles are stimulated by an outside agency. If, on the other hand, we take the word 'constraint' metaphorically, and say that the kleptomaniac is constrained, is under a psychological compulsion, to steal, then we lay ourselves open to the possibility that all our actions may be, in this sense, constrained. It is always dangerous for philosophers to establish their case by laying down what some key word means: they are liable to win themselves a hollow victory by definition, while the substance of the dispute eludes their grasp.

[1] See J. R. Lucas, *The Principles of Politics*, Oxford, 1966, Section 3 2 esp. pp. 144–146.

It is peculiarly fruitless when freedom and responsibility are under discussion. For if the sense of freedom is different from that connected with responsibility, the definition will be irrelevant: if it is tied to our concept of responsibility, it cannot carry with it a guarantee against possible redundancy, for our views about the conditions under which responsibility may properly be ascribed to a person have shifted, and may shift further, and might shift radically.

No simple linguistic thesis about the meaning of words can block the possibility that determinism may be relevant to responsibility. No philosopher is entitled to lay down *a priori* that it cannot be relevant. The traditional consensus of opinion is enough to establish a presumption the other way. And in arguments about the meanings of words public opinion is conclusive.

§5

DETERMINISM WITHOUT TEARS

THERE are many other arguments which claim to show us that we can be determinists without upsetting any of our notions of moral responsibility or human freedom. We may keep our concepts in different pockets. The language we use to describe actions is often different from the language we use to describe events: there are different principles of identity and individuation, for what are to count as the same action and what are to count as the same event. And therefore, it is argued,[1] the conflict between free-will and determinism is illusory, because the concepts occur in different languages and so cannot come into collision. Free-will belongs to the agent's language, determinism to the spectator's. I, as an agent, perform some actions freely: he, as a spectator, may predict events correctly. But I am not he; to be an active participator is not the same as to observe from the sidelines, and actions and events are logically very different; and therefore, it is claimed, no conflict can arise between my belief as an agent that I am acting freely and his certainty, as a spectator, that events will follow their pre-established course; since the key concepts of the opposition must be formulated in different languages, no contradiction between them can arise.

The distinction drawn between the language of agents and actions and the language of observations and events—a distinction which seems to be the modern formulation in linguistic terms of one that Kant[2] drew—is a distinction that needs to be drawn; but, like the one that Kant drew, is unable to resolve this particular problem. It is true that agents and spectators do use different languages, and many mistakes have been caused by the unconscious equation of actions and events: many of the legends

---

[1] For example, by P. F. Strawson and G. J. Warnock, in D. F. Pears, ed., *Freedom and the Will*, London, 1963, pp. 63–67.

[2] *Groundwork of the Metaphysic of Morals*, pp. 115–118, tr. H. J. Paton, *The Moral Law*, London, 1948, pp. 124–126.

about Oracles and the fulfilment of their prophecies to the confusion of the enquirer, turn on his having wrongly translated from
the Oracle's spectator-language into his own, agent-language. But
from the languages' not being the same in all respects it does not
follow that they differ in all respects. The languages, though admittedly different, overlap each other in many places. The same
man can speak both as an agent and as a spectator, and the same
things can be described from the two different points of view. Just
as Kant's solution requires a sort of philosophical schizophrenia
on the part of the thinker beyond the power of most reflective
men, so the solution suggested here requires, as it were, a
thorough-going schizoglossia which is blatantly at variance with
the facts. We may not be able to equate actions with events: but
we can say something in the event language which will translate
into something in the action language that is incompatible with
some things the agents would have liked to have been able to say.[1]
Thus I may think that my action in inviting the visiting professor
to dinner was free, and that I could have quite well just asked him
how his work was getting on: but if a psycho-physiologist with
complete information about the state of my brain and my environment at some previous time can predict that upon my meeting a
human being of such and such type, my lips will contort themselves so that such and such sounds come out, then, whatever the
niceties of what exactly constitutes an action, I shall no longer be
able to maintain that I could have not acted as I did. The argument of the two languages will not work because the spectator and
the agent can communicate, indeed may be the same person. So,
anything the spectator can know the agent could know also: and
if the spectator in his language can predict certain events, then
this state of affairs will be describable in the agent's language as
well, and may be inconsistent with, or entail, certain courses of
action on his part. Therefore if the determinist thesis occurs in
the spectator's language, it can be expressed in the agent's
language too, and the problem will not have been dissolved.

Professor MacKay, in a powerful and intriguing article, has
argued,[2] however, that in a sense the spectator and the agent

---

[1] See G. J. Warnock, "Actions and Events", in D. F. Pears, ed., *Freedom
and the Will*, London, 1963, pp. 75–78.

[2] D. M. MacKay, "On the Logical Indeterminacy of a Free Choice",
Mind, LXIX, 1960, pp. 31–40.

cannot communicate, because if they did, it would constitute an alteration in the situation which would make the spectator's prediction no longer applicable. There is a necessary secrecy about predictions of what an agent is going to do, and therefore it is improper to regard them as in any way revealing the "true state of affairs", and hence for the agent concerned "any proposition purporting to specify his choice in advance is simply *logically indeterminate* until he makes the choice". But secrecy surrounding predictions is not indubitably a necessary one. With some people—undergraduates, who, as a class, are highly countersuggestible—to communicate a prediction is to ensure its nonfulfillment. With others, who are more sure of themselves, it may make no difference, and with others again a prediction may make them act in the way predicted. More seriously, a spectator can make predictions on the basis of various different assumptions about the relevant state of affairs. He can predict what I shall do, supposing I am not told, but he may set about predicting what I shall do, supposing I am told I shall do X, or supposing I am told I shall do Y, or .... ; and it may be that he will predict that supposing I am told I shall do Z, I shall do Z. It may be. But perhaps it is not, because the Z in the prediction as communicated to the agent has to be the same as in the prediction as fulfilled by him. Perhaps it is like trying to jump on one's own shadow. The agent, at least if a countersuggestible one, might always be one step ahead of the predictions made about him and communicated to him.[1] The spectator in making his calculation would have to refer to the result in the course of making it, and there are valid grounds for doubting whether such a procedure is possible.[2] Yet it is, thus far, only a perhaps. Prediction-paradoxes are easy to construct, but persistently unconvincing. Later on, we shall produce a self-referential paradox which is incontrovertible,[3] and does not involve a perpetual chase after one's own tail.[4] MacKay's argument raises what will be the decisive issue against determinism, but is not itself conclusive.

Even if we allow MacKay's argument, and allow that the agent's view-point is necessarily different from that of the

[1] See K. R. Popper, "Indeterminism in Quantum Physics and Classical Physics", *British Journal for the Philosophy of Science*, **1**, 1951, pp. 179–188.   [2] See below, Section 22.
[3] Sections 24–29.   [4] Compare below, Section 27, p. 144.

spectator, it is difficult to accept his contention that it is just as good. For in retrospect, as MacKay himself admits,[1] the agent becomes a spectator, and will see that his action was predictable, and completely explicable in terms of external antecedent circumstances. He, like the other spectators, will see that he could not have done otherwise than he did do, and that his action did not really depend on him but was determined by antecedent external circumstances. His necessary ignorance of the prediction the spectators could make of what he was going to do, however necessary, was ignorance none the less. The agent's view-point, even if necessarily different, is not an autonomous one and cannot do more than preserve an illusion of freedom.[2]

It is sometimes claimed that we can give an analysis of responsibility which avoids the argument of the previous section[3] and does allow responsibility to be compatible with determinism. The traditional connexion between responsibility on the one hand, and praise and blame, reward and punishment, on the other, is reversed. Instead of saying that being responsible for an action is a necessary condition of a man's being justly praised or blamed, rewarded or punished for it, we are to define his being responsible as meaning that praise or blame, reward or punishment, are effective in causing him to do, or refrain from doing, that sort of action.[4] "A man is not punishable", says Nowell-Smith,[5] "because he is guilty; he is guilty because he is punishable, that is to say because some useful result is supposed to accrue from punishing him". And again[6] "The reason is we believe that the fear of punishment will affect the future behaviour of the thief but not that of the kleptomaniac."

The suggestion is implausible. We draw a sharp distinction between the questions of whether punishment is just and

---

[1] *op. cit.* p. 38n.

[2] See more fully, Allan M. Munn, *Free-will and Determinism*, London, 1960, Ch. VIII, pp. 208–210.

[3] pp. 14–16.

[4] Moritz Schlick, *Problems of Ethics*, tr. David Rynin, New York, 1939, Ch. VII, esp. Sections 5, 6, pp. 151–156. P. H. Nowell-Smith, "Freewill and Moral Responsibility", *Mind*, XLVII, 1948, pp. 45–60. The same argument was put forward a generation earlier by R. Blatchford, *Not Guilty*, London, 1906, pp. 161ff.

[5] p. 58.

[6] p. 60.

whether it is likely to be effective. There are occasions—under military law on the field of battle—where we "punish" people *pour encourager les autres*, without regard to whether it is just or not. But we regard such cases as exceptional, and think that there is a great difference between these and the normal cases. Whether or not a particular man could or could not have helped doing a particular action is not, in the common estimation of mankind, the same question as whether penalising him will discourage people in the same sort of situation from doing the same sort of action. We hold a kleptomaniac not responsible for his actions not because the fear of punishment will not deter—often it will—but because there are *other* indications of irrationality—"he steals one kind of article only—silk stockings or suspenders—and then proceeds to hoard them and not to resell."[1] As an account of what we mean by responsibility, the suggested analysis fails even to get off the ground.

It is, however, unhelpful to consider the suggestion on grounds of its plausibility. It should be regarded, rather, as a counter put forward by a philosopher already convinced of determinism, who then has to face the objection that the whole structure of moral judgement is based on the belief that men are free, and that if they are not, we shall no longer be able to make sense of our traditional concepts of praise and blame, and reward and punishment. The suggestion is really a salvage operation, to enable the convinced determinist to continue using the everyday concepts of praise, blame, reward, and punishment, or something very like them, in spite of his disbelief in freedom. Trying to define responsibility in terms of amenability to punishment constitutes on its own no argument in favour of determinism. But if we have other arguments in favour of determinism, then we might think it could be used to rebut a leading argument on the other side, the argument that freedom is presupposed by all our moral concepts. Even so, it does not achieve much. The initial implausibility is not dispelled by further examination. The more we look at it, the more artificial the suggested reconstruction of moral concepts becomes. Nobody is likely to find it satisfactory unless he is entirely convinced of determinism already: and anybody who is convinced, will not be greatly concerned to salvage moral judgement, and will be as ready to jettison it as to reform it. It is a suggestion which

[1] J. D. Mabbott, *An Introduction to Ethics*, London, 1966, p. 122.

will carry conviction only with the converted: and they will scarcely feel it worth bothering about.[1]

Another line of argument is to analyse freedom hypothetically, not categorically. A man was not free, or responsible for his actions, we are told, unless he could have done otherwise. But 'could have done otherwise' means not what we might think it means, but 'would have done otherwise if he had chosen'.[2] I am able to do Y = I would do Y if I chose to do it, and this is evidently compatible with my will's being so determined that I do not choose to do it.

The argument breaks down at a number of points.[3] Like the argument of the previous section, it suffers from the fundamental weakness of being based on an analysis of the meanings of words, and telling us in its conclusion that we do not mean what we think we mean. For we think that if any one could have known for certain in advance that the person in question was going to act in the way that he actually did, then he could not have not acted as he did; that is, he could not have acted otherwise. The deter-

---

[1] For fuller consideration see J. D. Mabbott, "Free Will and Punishment", *Contemporary British Philosophy*, 3rd series, ed. H. D. Lewis, London, 1956, pp. 289–309, esp. Section VI. See also, Isaiah Berlin, *Historical Inevitability*, Oxford, 1954, pp. 26–27n., reprinted in *Four Essays on Liberty*, Oxford, 1969, pp. 64–65n., and also the Introduction, pp. x–xxxvii.

[2] G. E. Moore, *Ethics*, London, 1912, 1966, Ch. 6; A. J. Ayer, "Freedom and Necessity", *Polemic*, 5, 1946, p. 43; reprinted in A. J. Ayer, *Philosophical Essays*, London, 1954, p. 282; P. H. Nowell-Smith, "Freewill and Moral Responsibility", *Mind*, LVII, 1948, Section 2, pp. 48–52. J. J. C. Smart, "Free-Will, Praise and Blame", *Mind*, LXX, 1961, pp. 298–303. C. L. Stevenson, *Ethics and Language*, New Haven, 1944, ch. XIV, pp. 298–318.

[3] See J. L. Austin, "Ifs and Cans", *Proceedings of the British Academy*, XLII, 1956, pp. 109–132; reprinted in J. L. Austin, *Philosophical Papers*, Oxford, 1961, pp. 153–180. But see also M. R. Ayers, "Austin on 'Could' and 'Could Have'", *Philosophical Quaterly*, 16, 1966, pp. 113–120. P. H. Nowell-Smith, "Ifs and Cans", *Theoria*, XXVI, 1960, pp. 85–101. D. J. O'Connor, "Possibility and Choice", *Proceedings of the Aristotelian Society*, Supplementary Volume XXXIV, 1960, pp. 1–24; Keith Lehrer, "Ifs, Cans and Causes", *Analysis*, XX, 1960, pp. 122–124; Richard Taylor, "I can", *Philosophical Review*, LXIX, 1960, pp. 78–89. D. Locke, "Ifs and Cans Revisited", *Philosophy*, XXXVII, 1962, pp. 245–256. For a very full consideration, see M. R. Ayers, *The Refutation of Determinism*, London, 1968.

minist interprets 'could' by reference to law-like propositions. Thus I could not have held my breath for five minutes to save my life, as we revealingly say, because there is a law of nature which precludes men holding their breath for five minutes; whereas I could quite well have not asked the visiting professor to dinner, because there is no law of nature from which it follows that men in my circumstances always ask visiting professors to dinner whenever they meet them in the street. To quote J. J. C. Smart:[1] "Suppose that when washing the dishes you drop a plate, but that fortunately it does not break. You say, however, that it *could* have broken. That is, within the range of possible initial conditions covered by possible cases of 'dropping', the known dispositional characteristics of the plate do not allow us to rule out the proposition 'it will break'. If, however, it had been an aluminium plate, then it could not have broken. That is, whatever the initial conditions had been (within a wide range) it would not have broken. Whether dropped flat or on its edge, with a spinning motion or with no spinning motion, from three feet or four feet or five feet, it still would not have broken. Thus such cases in which we use the words 'could have' or 'could not have' are cases in which we either cannot or can use a law or a law-like proposition to rule out a certain possibility despite our uncertainty as to the precise initial conditions."

The difficulty of this analysis of the word 'could' is that it deals with only one of several different senses in which the word is used. The word 'could', like the word 'can', is systematically ambiguous: it is used in several different, though related, ways, and the exact force of the word will change from context to context without any other indication of its alteration of sense. Within the particular sub-family of senses we are concerned with here, there is certainly one which answers to Smart's description: we sometimes use the words 'can' and 'could' to indicate simply the absence of laws or law-like propositions ruling out the possibility in question. But often also we use it to take into account not merely the relevant natural laws but some of the circumstances as well. This, indeed, is the sense Smart illustrates with his example of the plate. There is a wide range of circumstances which justify us in saying of the china plate that it could

[1] J. J. C. Smart, "Free-Will, Praise and Blame", *Mind*, LXX, 1961, p. 298.

have broken, and of the aluminium one that it could not have broken; but this is not so in all circumstances: if the floor had been covered with an inch-deep layer of foam-rubber, we should have retorted that the china plate could no more have broken than the aluminium one; 'could' here means 'could in the circumstances'. It is a very common use of 'could'. In politics and history for example, we often talk of what Caesar could have done, or discuss the choices open to Napoleon: but in such cases it is almost entirely the circumstances and hardly at all the laws of nature that give content to our propositions. No one doubts that in one sense Caesar could have stayed in his province or Napoleon not invaded Russia: but in another sense—taking into account the circumstances in which they were situated and the necessities of their positions—it can be argued intelligibly, though probably falsely, that they had no choice and, in another sense of 'could', could not have done otherwise. The sense of 'could' depends partly on our knowledge or laws or law-like propositions and the relevant circumstances. A mother comes to me in a great agitation because her younger son has eaten the contents of his brother's new chemistry set. 'They could be poisonous,' she weeps: 'No,' I assure her, 'Chemiboy chemistry sets are absolutely safe. A mixture of sulphur, sodium sulphate and calcium chloride is not going to hurt him.' I know more of the relevant circumstances than she, so that I can rule out possibilities which she can not. Therefore, though in one sense she can quite rightly use the word 'could', in another, and better, sense I can differ from her and use the words 'could not'. So also with plates, so also with men. If I am washing up for a Laplacian demon and drop a china plate and it does not break, I well might say with great relief that it could have broken: he, however, could correct me, and, making use of centres of percussion and moments of momentum, Hamiltonians and the equations of Lagrange, and coefficients of elasticity based on quantum mechanics with special reference to the solid state, might be able to prove conclusively that in the circumstances which actually obtained the plate could not have broken. I, through ignorance of the exact initial conditions, or through ignorance of the theory which showed what the relevance of the initial conditions was, had reached a wrong conclusion about what could happen in this particular case; and if I was reasonable, I should withdraw my assertion that the china plate could have broken, and accept the demon's correction with a good grace. Of course, I could, if I wanted, stick to my initial assertion and say that I meant 'It could have broken' just simply in the sense that it is not impossible for china plates to break when dropped: I can insist on being less precise than my information warrants. But to do so, once the more accurate information is available, is unreasonable: I might as well, when the aluminium plate was dropped, have exclaimed 'It could have broken' on account its being a domestic utensil and there being no law or law-like proposition ruling out the possibility of domestic utensils' breaking when dropped.

In the case of men, we can use 'could' and 'can' in Smart's sense, as when we say 'he could not have stayed under water for more than three minutes', 'he could not have scaled the walls of the prison'; these are the things which lie outside the capacities of the human race; nobody could do them, not even to save his life. The sense in which we normally use 'could' and 'can' in these contexts, however, is where we are concerned with a particular man placed in particular circumstances, and if the particular circumstances were such that it could have been predicted with certainty how the particular man was going to react to them, then there is a law-like proposition which rules out the possibility that the man in question in the circumstances would have acted otherwise, and this does warrant our saying 'he could not have acted otherwise'. This is the sense we use when considering moral responsibility. We exculpate a person who has acted under duress not because his action *per se* was one that no human being could help doing, but because it was one that nobody in his circumstances could help doing. We do not condemn a klepto-maniac in spite of the fact that there is no law or true law-like proposition which rules out the possibility of human beings not stealing, because we believe that a kleptomaniac is not simply a member of the human race but a member of a much smaller class of whom there is a true law-like proposition which does rule out the possibility of their not stealing. That is, in assessing moral responsibility we try and apply as specific laws as possible and take into account as many of the relevant circumstances as we can. For we want to be just in ascribing praise and blame, and justice is oriented towards the individual, and requires that we should consider all the features of the individual case. The sense of

3—F.O.T.W.

'could' in 'he could not have done otherwise' is therefore a strong sense, in which we use all the information available and concern ourselves specifically with the particular case in question. The problem is whether in the limit, when we know all the relevant information and apply all the operative natural laws, there will be any cases in which we shall conclude 'he could have done otherwise' in this "strong" sense of could. The libertarian believes that there will be: the determinist that there will not.

Many other arguments are put forward to show that determinism has no bearing on moral responsibility. I shall not discuss them in detail. They are light-weight. Nearly all of them start from the assumption that determinism is true, and seek to show how some parts of our thinking may nevertheless be salvaged. If determinism can be proved false, they are only of academic interest. Their only relevance for us is that they put the traditional assumption in question, and make it incumbent on us to show why, and in what sense, determinism is relevant to responsibility.

§6

DETERMINISM AND RESPONSIBILITY

THERE are two reasons why we feel that determinism defeats responsibility. It dissolves the agent's *ownership* of his actions: and it precludes their being really explicable in terms of their *rationale*. If determinism is true, then my actions are no longer really my actions, and they no longer can be regarded as having been done for reasons rather than causes.

It is a necessary condition of an action's being regarded as my own action, that it was up to me (in Greek, $\dot{\epsilon}\pi$' $\dot{\epsilon}\mu o\acute{\iota}$) whether or not I did it.[1] I could have decided not to do it, and if I had decided not to do it, it would not have been done, not by me at least. Constraint defeats responsibility, because even if I decided otherwise, even though I had decided otherwise, the *soi-disant* action would still take place. Determinism defeats responsibility, because it makes out that I could not have decided otherwise. Constraint makes my decision irrelevant: determinism makes it redundant. When I am constrained, my will can be left out of consideration, because what happens, happens willy-nilly: if I am determined, my will can be left out of consideration as an independent factor, because it can be calculated from the other factors already given. Constraint means I, my will, have nothing to do with the movement of my limbs: determinism means that I, my will, am otiose in accounting for the movement of my limbs. Although we can still account for my bodily movements as consequences of my will, we need not. We can equally account for them, as consequences of earlier conditions, making no mention of any decision of mine. Indeed better. For prediction involves time, and time makes the distinction between dependent and independent factors. So far as mathematical calculation goes, it is all one whether you calculate my decision from a set of other factors, or one of those other factors from the rest of them together with my decision. What makes the difference is that if

[1] Compare Aristotle, *Nicomachean Ethics* III, 1, 1110a17–18.

the other factors are all temporally antecedent to my decision, they cannot any of them be causal consequences of it. I cannot alter the past. At any date after the other factors and before my decision, the other factors are fixed and irrevocable. Therefore if there is a definite relation between them and my decision, it is my decision that is determined by them, not any of them by my decision. The direction of time settles the direction of dependence. There is a certain type of prediction which, if we can make it of any factor, makes that factor dependent, redundant and eliminable. If my decision is predictable in this way, it is no longer ἡ ἀρχὴ τοῦ κινεῖν, the starting point of action. The action no longer can be said to stem *from* my will, even though it may be mediated *through* it. And therefore it seems it is not really mine.

Men do not like redundancy. They like to feel that things depend on them, that they matter, that it makes a difference what *they* do. They do not like being taken for granted. Although they may pride themselves on being reliable and dependable, still they like to think that it is up to them whether they are or not; they want to reserve the right not to be. Else, they feel they are dispensable, not a factor to be reckoned with. Determinism deprives them of any real say in the course of events; not because they have a say, only, it is ineffective, but because they themselves, their very saying of their say, are totally dependent on other factors outside their control.

It is for these reasons that men do not like determinism, and feel that it poses a threat to their humanity. That is not enough to prove it false. Indeed, if it counts either way, it might be held to count in favour of determinism rather than against it, in as much as it can account for the common opinion against it as mere wishful thinking. But it does show us what the doctrines are that are in issue. The doctrines are ones that shake us, because they dissolve human agency into a set of other factors over which we have no control. And it is only with such shocking doctrines, which appear to eliminate the human element in the tide of events, that we need be concerned.

Determinism is felt to be a threat not only to humanity, but to rationality. For the sorts of explanations determinists think they can always give are, or are felt to be, incompatible with the sorts of explanation which justify, evaluate or assess actions. Some philosophers have denied the incompatibility, and it must be conceded that it is not self-evident that different types of explanation must necessarily exclude each other. Nor, however, is it self-evident that they must be compatible. The general feeling is that the sort of explanation offered by determinists is incompatible with normal explanations of actions, but the incompatibility has not been demonstrated. Only where there is some sort of incompatibility does any profound philosophical problem arise.

§7

PREDICTION

NOT every prediction poses a problem for freedom. Pupils never complain, if I, incautiously, predict for them a first, that I have circumscribed their freedom: and it is only modesty, and not a love of liberty, that makes me demur when others predict of me that I will pay my debts, tell the truth, and continue not to beat my wife. Fallible forecasts arouse no fears. A man may foretell what my future free decision will be, but so long as it is conceded that he may be wrong, I am narked by no necessity of having to make his forecasts come to pass. Many modern philosophers have confused themselves on this point. They have altered the meaning of 'predict' so that predictions cannot but come to pass, and continued to use the word in its previous range of applications, where we do speak of predicting, albeit fallibly, the future course of human affairs. We can guard against the confusion by always asking 'What would you say, supposing your prediction were not fulfilled?' If my pupil gets only a second, it just shows how incurably optimistic I am in assessing my pupil's abilities. If I tell a lie, or take to beating my wife, it just shows the frailty of the human heart. But if the perihelion of Mercury fails to remain constant, and we cannot find any further factor to account for it within the framework of Newtonian physics, then the whole theoretical fabric must fall. And so, contrapositively, since we are loth to abandon our favourite scientific theories, we are unready to envisage the possibility of predictions made with their aid ever being falsified. Hence the sense of necessity. It feels ineluctable only in as much as our statement of the initial conditions and of the natural laws invoked are believed to be certain. But most of our predictions make no pretensions to absolute certitude; and so pose no problem for freedom.

Sometimes I can feel certain about the future, because I know what I shall do. But I do not feel that my freedom is circumscribed. I am determining the future, rather than the future determining me.[1] Nor should I feel my responsibility eroded if another person made predictions about my future behaviour on the basis of my own avowals of intention. Predictions such as these, however certain, and however much they circumscribe the agent's freedom of action for the future, do not eliminate the agent's responsibility for his actions because they are not based entirely on independent factors outside his control. Even if we knew infallibly that a certain man, once having made a promise, could not break it, we still should not hold him not answerable for his performance of it, seeing that he need not have made it in the first place. It is only where predictions are based entirely on factors outside the agent's control that we feel that the actions predicted are themselves outside the agent's control, and therefore not really his at all. Most of the predictions we actually make are not like that; normally we predict a man's future actions on the basis of his past actions and avowals. It may shift back the originating decision, $\dot{\eta}$ $\dot{\alpha}\rho\chi\dot{\eta}$ $\tau o\hat{v}$ $\kappa\iota\nu\epsilon\hat{\iota}\nu$, but it does not put it outside the agent. Sometimes we specifically say that a man is the prisoner of his previous decisions, and say that he is not to be criticized on the score of what he is doing now in the situation into which he has got himself, but on account of his original decision, which landed him in his present predicament.

Most of our actual predictions about human actions profess both to be fallible and to be dependent on the agent concerned. There is nearly always the implicit hedge 'unless he changes his mind'. An undergraduate predicts that I shall be in my rooms on Wednesday at 10 to hear an essay from him, and on the strength of that prediction postpones going to the cinema on Tuesday, and devotes himself to preparing an essay. But although in one sense I may feel my freedom is circumscribed by my undertaking to him, and may regret, if the sun is shining invitingly at breakfast, that I am not free to spend the day roaming the countryside, neither the undergraduate nor I have the least inclination to say that my freedom of will has been removed by the prediction. The prediction is that I shall be in my rooms at 10 a.m. unless I change my mind, or something happens to prevent me being there. But if the conditions under which the prediction is made include that I

[1] See St. Augustine, *De Libero Arbitrio*, III, iii, 6–9; Stuart Hampshire and H. L. A. Hart, "Decision, Intention and Certainty", *Mind*, LXXI, 1958, pp. 1–12; Stuart Hampshire, *Thought and Action*, London, 1959.

do not change my mind, and that nothing happens to prevent me, on what grounds can I possibly contest, or object to, what is said? A prediction made only with the proviso that nothing should happen which might falsify it, is fail-safe. Either the prediction comes true, or it was not applicable. Either I do what you said I was going to do, in which case your prediction was correct: or I decide not to (or something happened to prevent me), but you had said that your prediction did not apply in such a case. What could be fairer than that? What could be more innocuous?

There are other predictions, however, which are not fail-safe, and which, if true, establish real limitations on our future freedom. You tell me I shall never levitate. My hopes of evidencing a particular sort of sanctity are thereby shattered, but not my human expectation of being able to arrange my ordinary actions as I will and not as you say. The freedom of the seas is real, even though ships are restricted to the surface, and cannot rise into the air or sail across land. The laws of mechanics, chemistry and thermodynamics can be said to circumscribe human freedom, and we may regret being restricted in the range of our choices: but such restrictions only limit, and do not deny, our liberty of choice. It is only if a complete specification of our actions, precise down to the last detail, can be calculated by means of scientific laws, that we feel our freedom is in jeopardy. Newtonian physics, by itself, made no threat to freedom by telling us what would happen if we were to fall freely under a gravitational force, and by laying down limits, through the principle of the conservation of energy, on what we could do: it was only when allied with Newtonian metaphysics, which viewed men as composed of corpuscles, all subject to Newtonian laws, that it seemed to leave no room for human choice. For then, from the initial positions and velocities of the corpuscles, Laplace could calculate with complete precision any subsequent state of the system. There would be nothing that Laplace could not know; and therefore, it was felt, no room for intervening choices to be effective.

We thus have three conditions which predictions must fulfil before they pose a threat to freedom: they must be infallible; they must be based on a limited range of factors, outside the agent's control; and they must be completely specific. Only those forms of determinism that claim to satisfy these conditions need worry us.

§8

CAUSES AND EXPLANATIONS

PREDICTION and explanation are linked. Indeed, according to Hempel,[1] prediction and explanation are but two sides of the same coin. This cannot be sustained for all types of prediction and all types of explanation,[2] though it is true enough for the types of prediction physical determinists believe in and the complete explanation they regard as the paradigm. But there are many other types of explanation, even more so than of prediction.

The concept of explanation is linked with that of cause, although not identical with it. The word 'because' shows the link. It characteristically is used to introduce an explanation, but often also seems to state the cause. Yet the word 'cause' in modern English does not always mean the same as 'explanation', and, more confusing still, the adjective 'causal' carries a different connotation from the noun 'cause'. Extreme caution must be exercised in using these terms. They are not always equivalent: but sometimes they are; and often they seem so. Much of the currently held case for determinism depends on an unconscious and illegitimate slide from one sense of one term to a different, and non-equivalent, sense of another.[3]

Explanations are answers. They are answers to questions, asked or anticipated, and in particular to the question 'Why?'. They characteristically begin with the word 'because', although we also explain what we are doing, who our friends are, and how we can bring our plans to fruition. We, however, are concerned

[1] C. G. Hempel, "The Function of General Laws in History", *The Journal of Philosophy*, **39**, 1942, esp. Section 4, pp. 38–39; reprinted in Herbert Feigl and Wilfrid Sellars, eds., *Readings in Philosophical Analysis*, New York, 1949, esp. p. 462.

[2] See, *e.g.*, N. R. Hanson, "On the Symmetry Between Explanation and Prediction", *Philosophical Review*, **68**, 1959, pp. 349–358.

[3] For example, that of Brand Blanshard, "The Case for Determinism", in Sidney Hook, ed., *Determinism and Freedom in the Age of Modern Science*, New York, 1958 and 1961. See below Section 11, pp. 51–64.

only with "why-because" explanations. They take many forms. Aristotle saw that the question 'Why?' and the answers it elicited were not always of the same type. His doctrine of the four Causes, or, as we might better say, of the four 'beCauses', specified four different types of explanation, types of explanatory answer which could be given.[1] Modern philosophers, in their non-metaphysical moods at least, are less procrustean and will admit a much wider variety of explanations than Aristotle's bare four. Anything counts as an explanation, we are sometimes inclined to say, provided it is felt to be explanatory of some problem, by some one, on some occasion: and even when we are less generous than that, we acknowledge a large number of different questions that can be answered in a large, possibly indefinitely large, number of different ways.

Not every type of explanation is a logically acceptable answer to every type of question. A scientist who is seeking a causal explanation and is given only a tautological one feels cheated; to explain the soporific effect of opium by saying that it possesses a *virtus dormativa* has long been recognized by scientists as no real answer to their query. Nevertheless, often a question admits of more than one answer, and it is unclear—perhaps even the questioner does not know—what sort of answer he is wanting. The word 'Why?' is in common use just because it is general and vague, and leaves the person furnishing the explanation free to give the sort of answer that he thinks will best satisfy the questioner. The questioner, just because he is a questioner, seeking enlightenment, is often not in a position to know the sort of answer he should be looking for. It is sensible not to specify too closely the answer his question is intended to elicit. We ask 'Why?' and wait till we have heard the answer before saying whether it is of a satisfactory sort or not.

It follows that there cannot be any exact account of explanation. Although it is not true that any answer will do, it is often the case that more than one answer might do, and we cannot lay down in advance exactly what answers are admissible in any given case. We rely not on antecedent specification of the answer required but on subsequent elucidation, by further question and answer, until a satisfactory one has been elicited. The questioner is offered first one, then another, and then another sort of answer,

[1] *Physics* II, 3,194b16–195b30; *Metaphysics* IV, 2,1013a24–1014a25.

until it is clear what it is that is puzzling him, and what sort of answer he is seeking. In practice it is flexible and effective, but it makes for incoherence and clumsiness in theory.

Although explanations are to some extent *ad hominem*, they are not entirely subjective. In spite of the promptings of philosophical liberalism, we will not allow anything to count as a satisfactory explanation, provided only that it is felt, by some one, on some occasion, to be explanatory of some problem. Not every answer that is accepted should be. There are some standards— although we cannot say what they are. But still, there are some standards: not every explanation is as good as every other.

Explanations, however dependent on the question they are answering and the questioner they are intended to illuminate, are open to rational criticism and assessment. What criticisms and assessments are reasonable remains a wide open question: it depends on our view of reason.[1] But at least it is not totally subjective, totally arbitrary or totally irrelevant. It must be based on some intersubjective, common ground, and must to that extent be of some degree of generality.

These are the only requirements we can lay down for all sorts of answers beginning with 'because': a logical one, that they are, at least covertly, general; and an epistemological one, that they are in some way related, through the rest of human knowledge, with the question asked. These requirements are very loose. Many bad explanations, as well as good ones, satisfy them. And therefore we are inclined to say that explanations, really to count as causes, should conform to these requirements in a more stringent version, and we come to regard causal explanations, as we term them, as being paradigms of what explanations ought to be. The argument is very fairly given by K. J. W. Craik:[2]

It is possible that the meaning of 'explanation' is different for different people; it may be one of those things which no one really understands, but which every scientist, or any one else in a mood of curiosity, feels he desires. His particular ideal, felt rather than known, determines the kind of experiments he will choose to do, and the kind of answer he will accept. Nevertheless, there is a large field of explanation that is common to most men. Explanations are not purely subjective things;

[1] See J. R. Lucas, "The Philosophy of the Reasonable Man", *The Philosophical Quarterly*, **13**, 1963, pp. 97–106.
[2] *The Nature of Explanation*, Cambridge, 1943, pp. 6–7.

they win approval or have to be withdrawn in the face of evidence and criticism; and the man who can explain a phenomenon understands it, in the sense that he can predict it, and utilise it more than other men.

The question why one explanation or another should seem satisfactory involves the prior question why any explanation at all should be sought after and found satisfactory. It is clear that, in fact, the power to explain involves the power of insight and anticipation, and that this is very valuable as a kind of distance-receptor in time which enables organisms to adapt themselves to situations which are about to arise. Apart from this utilitarian value, it is likely that our thought processes are frustrated by the unique, the unexplained and the contradictory and that we have an impulse to resolve this state of frustration, whether or not there is any practical application.

Craik is careful to allow that men have other than utilitarian motives for seeking explanations, and possibly other than utilitarian tests for assessing them. Nevertheless, those explanations that are associated with definite predictions have a pre-eminent place. Quite apart from their practical value, they are open to testing, and hence to rational assessment in a much more definite fashion than any other. It is tempting, on purely intellectual grounds, to specify the logical requirement, of generality, as demanding that the event to be explained shall be characterized as an instance of some universal rule, and to specify the epistemological requirement, of relevance, as demanding that the universal rule cited shall be susceptible of some definite empirical test. These two specifications characterize the "Covering Law" or "Regularity" schema of explanation, put forward by C. G. Hempel, and widely accepted by modern philosophers, as the paradigm for all explanation.

§9

REGULARITY AND RATIONAL EXPLANATIONS

ACCORDING to Hempel[1] the scientific explanation of the occurence of an event of some specific kind E at a certain place and time consists of

(1) a set of statements asserting the occurrence of certain events $C_1 \ldots C_n$ at certain times and places,
(2) a set of universal hypotheses, such that
    (a) the statements of both groups are reasonably well confirmed by empirical evidence,
    (b) from the two groups of statements the sentence asserting the occurrence of event E can be logically deduced.

Group (1) describes the initial and boundary conditions for the occurrence of the final event; group (2) contains the general law on which the explanation is based.[2] We shall need to amplify this account later,[3] but for the present it is quite adequate.

Hempel's account explicates fairly well what we mean when we talk, in ordinary life, of giving "the causes" of an event. In spite of Collingwood's protests,[4] the word 'cause' in modern English has come to be largely reserved for explanations (or better, parts of explanations[5]) which can be fitted into Hempel's schema. More especially when we talk of "causal explanations",

---

[1] C. G. Hempel, "The Function of General Laws in History", *The Journal of Philosophy*, **39**, 1942, pp. 35–48; reprinted in Herbert Feigl and Wilfrid Sellars, eds., *Readings in Philosophical Analysis*, New York, 1949, pp. 459–471.

[2] p. 36; or pp. 459–460.   [3] In Section 17.

[4] R. G. Collingwood, *An Essay on Metaphysics*, Oxford, 1940, Chs. XXIX–XXXIII, pp. 285–337.

[5] J. R. Lucas, "Causation", in *Analytical Philosophy*, 1st series, ed. R. J. Butler, Oxford, 1962, esp. Section III, pp. 54–63; see also R. G. Collingwood, *op. cit.*, p. 286 and pp. 296–312.

even (useful, because ugly) of "causal causes", we have Hempel-type explanations in mind. But Hempel does not think he is explicating only one type of explanation. Although he introduces his schema as an account of scientific explanation, he goes on to argue that it is the only type of explanation to deserve the name, and that any alleged explanation which cannot be fitted into his schema is only a "pseudo-explanation". In particular, he claims that historical explanations are, in principle, no different from his scientific ones;[1] and many people feel that he must be right.

It is partly a simple confusion in the use of the word 'scientific'. Sometimes it is used as opposed to 'unscientific', sometimes as opposed to 'non-scientific'. In the first sense it is synonymous with 'rational', in the second it is confined to the natural sciences. An explanation which is not scientific in the first sense—an unscientific explanation—may well be adjudged a pseudo-explanation, no explanation at all. But it does not follow that an explanation which is not scientific in the second sense is not really an explanation, unless we are prepared to maintain, what is patently false, that the only knowledge we do, or can, have is that derived from the natural sciences. We can use the word 'science' in either sense, but not in both at once. We can use it, as in the Middle Ages, to mean any rational discipline, any reputable body of knowledge: then to say of an explanation offered by a historian that it was unscientific would be a serious, well-nigh fatal, criticism: but the criteria of what constitutes a scientific explanation are difficult to formulate and apply. Or we can use the word 'scientific' to distinguish what goes on in laboratories, as opposed to what goes on in libraries and elsewhere. It will then be usually possible to reach agreement on whether a particular activity, argument or answer is a scientific one or not: but to deny to the date of the Battle of Hastings the status of scientific fact will be merely to classify correctly, and not in any way to downgrade it.

Apart from this confusion, there are the two requirements outlined in the previous section,[2] that explanations must be in some way general, and that they must be related with the rest of knowledge. These requirements are made more stringent by the Hempelians. They assume that the only way in which causes can be general is that they should be instances of general laws. The

[1] pp. 39–40; p. 463.   [2] p. 35.

covert generality implicit in the word 'because' can be satisfied, it is felt, only if we can state a universal hypothesis, whose antecedent "covers" the putative cause, and whose consequent "covers" the event to be explained. But this, although a way of satisfying the requirement of generality, is not the only way. All that rationality, claimed by the use of the word 'because', requires is a weak principle of universalisability, not the strong. That is, if I offer an explanation to a questioner, and he produces a *prima facie* parallel case for which the explanation will not work, I must be able to show what the difference between the two cases is: but I do not have to be able to specify exactly in advance the features of the event to be explained and the proffered cause, and an exactly specified universal hypothetical statement connecting them. The strong and the weak requirements of universalisability differ in the order of the quantifiers. The strong requirement is that I should specify some general features $C_1, C_2, \ldots, C_n; E$ such that for all cases x, if the antecedent situation is characterized by conditions $C_1, C_2, \ldots, C_n$, then it will have the further feature E, that an event of the type in question will occur within a given time. In symbols

$$(\exists C_1)(\exists C_2) \ldots (\exists C_n)(\exists E)(x): C_1(x) \,\&\, C_2(x) \,\&\ldots\&\, C_n(x) . \supset E(x).$$

The weak requirement, however, reverses the quantifiers. It merely requires that for any case put forward where the explanation does not work there must be some differentiating feature D whose absence explains why the explanation does not hold in this case. That is, for any case x, such that

$$C_1(x) \,\&\, C_2(x) \,\&\, \ldots \,\&\, C_n(x) \,\&\, \sim E(x)$$

there is a further feature D, such that $\sim D(x)$.

We can express this requirement positively,

$$(x)(\exists C_1) \ldots (\exists C_n)(\exists D)(\exists E): C_1(x) \,\&\, \ldots \, C_n(x) \,\&\, D(x) . \supset E(x).$$

In the weak requirement of universalisability the universal quantifier comes before the existential ones: it is therefore not equivalent to the strong requirement of universalisability.[1]

[1] Compare the difference between the true proposition that for every number there is another larger and the false proposition that there is a number larger than every other number. The former could be expressed $(x)(\exists y)R(x,y)$ where $R(x,y)$ means that y is a number greater than x: the latter could be expressed $(\exists y)(x)[x \neq y \supset R(x,y)]$. For a fuller exposition see J. R. Lucas, "The Lesbian Rule", *Philosophy*, XXX, 1955, pp. 195–213.

Rationality requires universalisability only in the weak sense. Universalisability in the strong sense, while meeting, and more than meeting, the demands of rationality, is a characteristic requirement of the natural, and more especially the physical, sciences. If, therefore, we fail to distinguish the two senses of universalisability, we are easily led to demand of all explanations something that is typical only of scientific (in the modern sense) ones; and hence to assimilate all explanations to the Hempelian pattern.

Hempel is quite explicit about the second requirement. He urges that an "explanation of scientific character is amenable to objective checks", among them "an empirical test of the universal hypotheses on which the explanation rests".[1] The epistemological requirement that the explanation shall be related through the rest of human knowledge with what it purports to explain, has been tightened up to the requirement that the barest statement of the relation shall be by itself amenable to a direct empirical test. This is the Verification Principle in a strong form. All that relevance requires is a very weak Verification Principle. An explanation is irrelevant if it has no bearing on what it purports to explain, or has no connexion with the rest of human knowledge. If it would make no difference, so far as the questioner can find out, whether the explanation actually offered had been given or its negation, then he may reasonably reject it as idle. But the difference it makes does not have to be susceptible of immediate empirical test. Even in the natural sciences there are many theoretical statements which cannot be subjected to an immediate empirical test: when faced with a counter-example, we often have a choice of which statements in our theory we shall amend or reject: and our choice may be guided by non-empirical, though still objective, considerations. Much more so in the humanities. There are innumerable different ways in which an explanation may be related to what it purports to explain, and these may be rationally assessed and criticized, although often we depend on a consensus of opinion, rather than any definite decision-procedure, to settle whether a suggested explanation will stand or not. All that we are entitled to demand at the outset is that totally subjective explanations are barred. To that extent, we may stipulate that an explanation should be "amenable to

[1] *Op. cit.*, p. 38; pp. 461–462.

objective checks". But these checks need not be, although they may be, empirical tests. As Craik puts it, "Explanations are not purely subjective things; they win approval or have to be withdrawn in the face of evidence *and criticism.*"[1] Provided that there is some criticism, some argument—not necessarily a piece of evidence or the result of an experiment—which will tell in favour or against an explanation, and which is in some way connected with the rest of human knowledge, the explanation is not to be ruled out of court at the very beginning. Thereafter it may be a difficult and detailed dispute whether a particular explanation is satisfactory or not. We cannot give any general rules. Certainly we are not entitled to demand that the strong Verification Principle should apply in every case. Once again, there has been a needless transition from a weak requirement which we can reasonably expect all respectable explanations to satisfy, to a strong one which is characteristically satisfied only by explanations in the natural sciences.

There is thus no justification for the claim that all explanations, if genuinely explanatory, must be susceptible of the Hempelian analysis. Nor is it true. Many of the explanations which we give in answer to the question 'Why?' and which are accepted by the general run of questioners as satisfactory, do not seem to fit Hempel's schema. Nor, despite persistent efforts carried out with much ingenuity,[2] has it proved possible to exhibit even historical explanation as conforming to the Hempelian pattern.[3] We therefore should reject Hempel's claim to have portrayed the paradigm of all explanation, while conceding that he has given the explication of one, very important, type. We could call it "causal explanation", but in order to avoid unnecessary use of possibly misleading terms, I shall call it "regularity explanation". For it explains the occurrence of an event of some specific kind E at a certain place and time, by citing, in virtue of some regularity, the occurrence of some other specific conditions, $C_1, C_2, \ldots, C_n$, at certain related places and times, which reveal the occurrence of the event of type E as a typical instance of that regularity.

Regularity explanations are of great importance: but there are many others. Formal explanations—the successors to Aristotle's

---

[1] *Op. cit.*, p. 7 (quoted above pp. 35–36); my italics.
[2] P. L. Gardiner, *The Nature of Historical Explanation*, London, 1952.
[3] W. H. Dray, *Laws and Explanations in History*, London, 1957.

4—F.O.T.W.

Formal Causes—are those where we explain a proposition—*e.g.*
'Why is 257 a prime number?'—by deducing it from other
propositions, and ultimately from ones that are either analytic or
postulated as axioms. The term 'rational explanations' I reserve
for the successors, and more, of Aristotle's Final, or Teleological,
Causes. Any explanation I can give in justification of my
actions is a rational explanation. Sometimes, when it can be
expressed by means of a final clause—'I did it in order to earn
some money'—, it is a Final or Teleological explanation; but
often, when the justification is not in terms of some end to which
the action in question was conducive, we invite confusion by
using the terms 'Final' or 'Teleological'. Thus 'Because she is
old and lonely' is a rational explanation of my action in going to
see her, but not a teleological one.

Rational explanations are two-faced. They give the reasons
why *I did* the action in question, but also reasons why *one should*.
The latter need not be, although they may be, moral reasons.
Any reasons, moral, prudential, intellectual, aesthetic, or any
other, may be given, provided only that they make my action
intelligible to the questioner. He needs to be brought to understand how I came to act as I did. The reasons I give must be *my*
reasons—else I am rationalising, not giving my real reasons—,
but they must be *reasons* which could be reasons for him—else
my action will remain opaque and unexplained. In accepting my
reasons as reasons which could be reasons for him, the questioner
does not have to accept them as morally cogent or as the only
relevant reasons. He may understand, and still condemn. To explain my action may not be, in the ordinary sense, to justify it.
But it must begin to justify. If I give as a reason for my action
something which could never lead the questioner to think of
doing it in any circumstances, under any description, then my
reason will not explain to him at all why I acted as I did. It is only
because my actual reasons are ones which he could conceive as
being, under some conditions, reasons why he should have acted
similarly, that my stating them helps him to understand why I
acted on them.[1]

The reason why rational explanations may explain without
completely justifying, is that practical reasoning is, like many
other sorts of reasoning, *dialectical*. Characteristically, although

[1] For a fuller discussion, see W. H. Dray, *op. cit.*, ch. V.

not always, there are "two sides to the case". There are arguments for a proposed course of action, and arguments against. We have a choice of either doing one action, for which there are some arguments, or doing an alternative, for which there are other arguments. We have to ponder and deliberate, balancing the *pros* and *cons*, weighing the respective advantages of the alternatives. Therefore the argument is two-sided. And so it is that a questioner can understand my explanations without accepting them as justifications. My reasons were reasons indeed, supporting a decision one way; and so he understands me: but there were other reasons, supporting a decision the other way, which I ought, he reckons, to have found decisive; and so he condemns me. Over human actions, and in the humanities generally, we can enter into a man's reasoning without endorsing it: although where we have no sympathy at all, and could not conceivably endorse, then neither can we understand.

Rational explanations are radically different from regularity ones. Rational explanations satisfy only the weak requirement of universalisability and the weak Verification Principle, whereas regularity explanations satisfy the strong requirement of universalisability and the strong Verification Principle. So far as our ordinary life and ordinary discourse are concerned, we employ both types of explanation, as well as many others. In our metaphysical moods we may feel that only one type of explanation should be admitted as really explanatory, and that all others must be squeezed into, or reduced to, the favoured form. But such procrustean programmes need cogent arguments to be adduced in their support.

§10

PARTIAL AND COMPLETE EXPLANATIONS

LIFE is brief. Our answers are best brief too. We offer the explanation which we think will be most helpful to the questioner, and do not attempt to answer all the questions that a person in his position might have in mind. Our explanations are characteristically *partial* explanations, which may need to, and can, be filled out by further questions and answers in the subsequent discussion. We try and tell the questioner what he does not know, or has not thought of, or has not understood, and not the many other things which he does know or understand, and without which our answer would be unintelligible. We do not explain a broken window to an irate house-holder by telling him that glass is brittle, but by identifying, if possible, the boy who threw the stone: whereas the dermatologist does not tell the nurse with a skin-rash, what she knows already, that she had been administering penicillin to patients, but tells her, rather, the law-like statement that penicillin on her skin provokes a rash. In each case, it is only because the questioner knows something, in fact many things, that we can furnish him with some further fact or consideration which will be illuminating and helpful to him. Our explanation provides the final clue, but does not attempt to tell the whole story.

Partial explanations may seem to conflict when they do not really. Many factors combine to account for the feature that puzzles us, and different informants may select different factors as being the ones we most need to know or the ones we should take to be the most important. The murder at Sarajevo led to the First World War, but only because of many other conditions, which we want to be told about. We may go further, and think that the murder at Sarajevo was less important than some other factor or factors. We may even argue about it. But, if we do, our arguments are arguments about emphasis rather than about anything else, and it is possible for both parties to the argument to be right. Different emphases are required on different occasions or for different purposes. Two partial explanations may be partial selections from the same complete explanation, differently selected for different purposes, or for the benefit of different sorts of questioner.

Different partial explanations of the same problem can thus be reconciled, if they both can be supplemented towards the same complete explanation. We can account for the difference as a difference of emphasis, while maintaining that at bottom there is no real disagreement. When all the cards are on the table, both parties are found to have the same hand, and the order in which they were produced can be regarded as immaterial. It often happens in discussion that each party ends up agreeing with all the chief points made by the other, and differing only, if at all, in the emphasis to be put on them. We can reasonably conceive this as the ideal end-point of amicable argument. Although at the outset, different and apparently rival explanations were in the field, the difference was due not to a substantial disagreement but to a different choice of what should be said and what left unsaid. Our necessarily elliptical mode of speech highlights any differences of emphasis there may be, while concealing the underlying substantial agreement. Therefore, if we are to reconcile different partial explanations, and to give a single, coherent and adequate explanation, it should be a *complete* explanation, leaving nothing unsaid, and instancing every relevant factor or consideration.

Partial explanations, because they are partial, are often difficult to classify. If to the question 'Why did you hit him?' I answer 'Because he hit me', it may be unclear whether I am giving a rational explanation or a regularity one.[1] I may be adducing the fact that he hit me as a reason why one should have hit him: or I may be citing it and assuming the general law *si on l'attaque, il se defende*, to give a regularity explanation—a causal explanation—of the blow. The short answer does not always fix the precise sort of explanation: further questions may be needed to elucidate exactly how the initial answer is to be understood, and in their absence we may be tempted to misconstrue it. This is particularly so with the explanation of actions. For a rational explanation of

[1] See G. J. Warnock, in D. F. Pears, ed. *Freedom and the Will*, London, 1963, p. 61.

an action must, if sufficiently fully detailed, include some features of the situation in which it was enacted: the explanation has to show that it was a reasonable thing to do *in those circumstances*; and, clearly, what is appropriate in one set of circumstances is inappropriate in some others. Therefore a partial rational explanation of an action may consist simply of citing some circumstance or feature of the situation in virtue of which the action was a reasonable one to do. But to cite an antecedent condition is typical of regularity explanations. And so, many philosophers have been led to confound the two. If they seek for the "causes" they can always find some antecedent conditions because of which they acted as they did, and conclude therefore that their actions are always susceptible of a causal, that is to say a regularity, explanation. Only if we fill out our explanations of our actions, do we find that usually the causes they instance are not causal but rational 'becauses'.

Explanations in every day life are not static, not always quite all right just as they are, but partial, and often in need of being supplemented or replaced by another. The context of question and answer is a dynamic one, which enables us, and on occasion requires us, to move from one explanation to another. Quite apart from philosophical predilections, we have an urge on occasion to amplify explanations, and a hankering for complete explanations which need no further filling out. It is not metaphysical madness but an entirely normal procedure to seek to go from one explanation to another, better. Even in ordinary life one explanation occasionally, but importantly, replaces another in a strong sense. Rationalisations are putative reasons which the agent adduces to explain and justify his action, and which he may well believe were really the reasons for which he acted, but which, according to a different and deeper account, were merely window-dressing: according to the revised account, the man's action is to be explained in terms of some other motive, which by itself was enough to account for the action, and the alleged "reasons" had nothing to do with it at all. The agent's explanation has been edged out and replaced by one which leaves no room for it.

On other occasions explanations are replaced not by being pushed out, but by being incorporated into, the explanation which replaces them. Thus the Kinetic Theory of Gases explains the elasticity of gases in terms of the Newtonian concepts of the mass, momentum, and velocity of the molecules of gas. We can still explain phenomena in terms of the pressure of a compressed gas, but if we are on our best behaviour, and are giving the fullest and most adequate explanation that we can, we shall go behind such crudities, and reduce them to their fundamental terms. The scientist, in particular, seeks to explain what hitherto had been unexplained: he often will seek explanations of what has been tendered in explanation of something else; and if he is successful, we no longer offer the old explanation, but in its place the new one, in which the explanation itself has been explained.

So much for ordinary life. In philosophy we acquire ambitions. We want to lay down a list of correct, effective, acceptable, satisfactory, explanatory explanations; and we want to explain not just particular things, partially, *ad quendam hominem*, but everything, completely, to every comer. We seek the *real* explanation of things, the ultimate or the fundamental explanation, in terms of which all other explanations can themselves be explained. We do not necessarily deny that there are other, less fundamental types of explanation; at the least, we must allow that they are felt to be explanatory, and we may even allow that they *are* explanatory to some extent. But they are not ultimately satisfactory. They need to be based on, or they can be reduced to, another, more fundamental form of explanation, and it is this most fundamental form of explanation that we, as metaphysicians, are interested in.

There cannot be more than one most fundamental form of explanation. Metaphysicians who think they have found the fundamental form, will have to assimilate, incorporate, reduce, or explain away, all other types of explanation. Metaphysics apart, it is not obvious whether we can have more than one complete explanation of the same thing. Leibniz and Kant maintained we could: but most people feel we cannot. Certainly some types of complete explanation are incompatible with there being any other explanation of some other sort. We cannot have both a complete formal and any regularity explanation. A formal explanation, we may say, developing Aristotle's account, is a tautological one. Plato's theory of Forms sought to explain everything in such a way. The reason why a beautiful thing is beautiful is that it participates in the Form of Beauty, and so in every case.[1] Plato explicitly put forward his theory of Forms as a rival to the theories

[1] *Phaedo*, 100C.

of scientific explanation he had accepted in his youth, and it is just because it leaves no room for scientific or causal (*i.e.* regularity) explanation that we object to it. A tautological explanation is too good. It leaves no room for contingency, no room for possible error. Plato has made explanations in terms of his theory of Forms unfalsifiable, and therefore it does no explanatory work in explaining empirical phenomena. In mathematics and formal logic we can accept complete formal explanations: we can give a complete explanation of why 257 is a prime number, or $\sqrt{2}$ is irrational, or the monadic predicate calculus is decidable, in purely deductive terms. But, for this very reason, we cannot give any regularity or causal explanation. Having given a complete formal explanation, we have left no room for any further explanation whatever. We have said what there is to be said: there is nothing further we can say, which will not either be irrelevant, or repeat, or contradict, what we have already said. Plato's theory of explanation necessarily excludes explanations of any other sort, and in particular regularity ones; and therefore fails to satisfy any one who thinks that regularity explanations must be given of empirical phenomena.

It might be thought that there is no difference between formal and complete regularity explanations; since on the account we have given, complete regularity explanations are deductive too. But, unlike the complete formal explanations we have been considering, a regularity explanation always can fail, in either of two ways: the generalisation cited may not in fact be true; or the initial conditions may not have been as stated. We are always prepared in the end, though often with great reluctance, to abandon a putative law of nature if it is falsified by the facts: and often there is room for doubt whether initial conditions have been accurately specified. In practice, of course, we know that we do not know the initial conditions perfectly, and often have not succeeded in formulating the general law properly and fully. But even in principle we are prepared to give way, for preference over the initial conditions, but if necessary over the general law itself. And therefore we are putting forward an explanation which, falsifiable in principle, has enough elbow-room for it to be able to explain contingent experience.

A complete teleological explanation seems equally to preclude any real regularity explanation in causal terms, in spite of

Leibniz's endeavour to construct a metaphysics that was both teleological and causal.[1] If we believe in the providential ordering of things so completely that every single event is "meant", we no longer can explain things usefully by reference to (causal) causes: for the causes too were "meant", were what they were just in order to bring about the results that followed.

There seems to be a similar incompatibility between a complete regularity explanation and there being any rational one. For they have different logics. Complete regularity explanations operate with the traditional "monologous" deductive logic, whereas rational explanations, like rational arguments, are typically dialectical in form: they are never complete; they cannot, without distortion, be sewn up and presented in water-tight deductive form, for there is always the possibility of a further 'but' to be advanced and considered before a conclusion can be drawn.[2] Quite apart from the special logic of rational explanation, it seems to follow from there being a complete causal explanation of something that no other explanation of it could be admitted, except in a merely derivative capacity. If we have given a complete regularity explanation of everything, there is nothing else for any rational explanation to explain: and if some other explanation were to explain exactly the same things, but in a different way, since it has to explain exactly the same things, it is going to be exceedingly difficult for it to be a different, autonomous explanation: for if it were, it might be an explanation of a slightly different set of things; in which case it would either be wrong or else be a weaker explanation, explaining things less exactly than the paradigm complete regularity explanation does. Kant's two standpoints do not succeed in resolving the problem. Even if one could assess things morally, in spite of the fact that they were determined causally, there would be no practical point in any human being doing so, since his actions would be, if completely explicable in regularity terms, determined. Or, looking at it the other way round, it must be possible that something which is

[1] See for example, his *Discourse on Metaphysics*, Ch. XIX and Ch. XXII.
[2] For a similar argument, see A. C. MacIntyre, "Determinism", *Mind*, LXVI, 1957, pp. 34–35. The argument given here is not open to the objections which could be raised against MacIntyre's version. See further below, Section 16, pp. 88–89.

going to happen is not the best of all possible outcomes, and therefore that one ought to act so as to better the outcome: and therefore a moral agent must introduce an element of unpredictability, something not susceptible of a complete regularity explanation.

GENERAL ARGUMENTS FOR AND AGAINST DETERMINISM

THE chief general arguments for determinism turn on ideas, often confused, of explicability. Provided we take reasonable care to distinguish the different senses of 'explanation', 'cause' and 'causal', we see that the arguments do not really hold at all.

Historians are sometimes determinists, because they confuse partial and complete explanations. They are committed to explaining historical events, and explanation, they feel, involves determination. If a historian can explain why an event took place, he is explaining why it must have taken place. For he is explaining why the event in question took place, and not any other. And if no other event could have taken place, then the event that did take place must have taken place, and determinism is true. An explanation which does not have deterministic implications is less than complete, and therefore less than satisfactory. The only libertarian history is incomplete history. Only the idle or incompetent historian can avoid aspiring to be a determinist.

Historical determinism takes many forms. The Marxist claims that economic factors alone determine the course of history, and are themselves governed by the definite laws of dialectical materialism. Even those historians who reject the crudities of Marxism are liable to the feeling that some set of factors, not necessarily economic, determines the course of history, and that the decisions of the individual play no real part. It may be just a feeling of impotence and the recalcitrance of human affairs. "I pondered," said William Morris ". . . how men fight and lose the battle, and the thing they fought for comes about in spite of their defeat, and when it comes turns out to be not what they meant, and other men have to fight for what they meant under another name": often this feeling is cast in metaphysical form, and a theory of historical determinism propounded.

The argument turns on the nature of historical explanation.

It assumes that a satisfactory explanation must not only show why the event in question took place, but why no other event could have taken place. But actual explanations offered by historians seldom do this. Often they are not of the "Why necessarily" form, but of the "How possibly".[1] Even those explanations which explain why, do not reveal a necessity that precludes freedom. In explaining why a man did something we may give, or reconstruct, his reasons. But reasons are seldom all one way. Usually there are arguments on both sides, some for the proposed action, some against: if not, the action hardly needs explaining. Where there are arguments on both sides, we can explain the man's decision by recounting the arguments on that side: but if he had decided against the action, we could have then explained his decision to the contrary, by recounting the arguments on the other side. Either way we could have given an explanation. In each case the explanation would have explained why the alternative action was not undertaken. But in neither case would it have shown that the agent had to act the way he did, and was unable to act otherwise. We give his reasons in each case, and his reasons show why he should have acted as he did; but not that, in the relevant sense of 'could', he could not have acted otherwise. Historical explicability fails to yield determinism, because a characteristic historical explanation is not a complete one, and the reasons adduced are not outside the agent's control. It is up to him whether he regards them as cogent, or some factor on the other side as decisive. We may ask the further question, why did such and such a person regard such and such reasons as good ones; but that is a different question[2] and one that historians do not normally seek to answer. It is difficult enough to tell us how things happened and show us the reasons why people acted as they did, without presuming to prove that nothing could have happened otherwise than it did.

Besides confusing partial with complete explanations, people often confuse explanations of different types. Many thinkers affirm a principle of universal causation, that Every Event has a Cause. If we take the word 'cause' to mean 'causal cause' (*i.e.*

---

[1] See W. H. Dray, *Laws and Explanation in History*, Oxford, 1957, Ch. VI; or W. H. Dray, "Explanatory Narrative in History", *The Philosophical Quarterly*, 4, 1954, pp. 15–27.

[2] See further below, Section 29.

regularity cause) as seems reasonable, then granted certain conditions,[1] the principle is a determinist one. But when pressed to justify the principle of universal causation, its proponents interpret it to mean that every event has an explanation. This is a different principle, and a much easier one to maintain. If the word 'cause' means simply 'explanation', then it may well be true that every event has a cause, but it carries no determinist implications: if it means cause in the strict regularity sense, then it is far from self-evident that every event has a cause.

The argument is particularly seductive when applied to human actions. For it is characteristic of actions that the agent can say why he did them. If we think of our actions, we can usually remember why we did them, and assign as "causes" (*i.e.* partial explanations) some antecedent condition; and then interpret these causes as causal causes, as parts of complete regularity explanations.[2] Blanshard[3] tells of Sir Francis Galton, who "kept account in a notebook of occasions on which he made important choices with a full measures of [the] feeling of freedom; then shortly after each choice he turned his eye backward in search of constraints[4] that might have been acting on him stealthily. He found it so easy to bring such constraining factors to light that he surrendered to the determinist view." "You are too much pre-occupied," he tells the reader ". . . to give any attention to the causes of which your choice may be an effect. But that is no reason for thinking that if you did preoccupy yourself you would not find them at work."

Many besides Sir Francis Galton have been convinced of the truth of determinism by this line of reasoning. But once we distinguish different types of explanation, the spring of the argument is broken. From the fact that an action is explicable, it does not follow that it is determined, in the sense in which we are using the word 'determined'. I refuse an invitation. You ask me to think why I refused. On reflection I say that it was because the last time I went to a party, I found it very boring. The boringness

---

[1] See Section 7, p. 32.

[2] See above, Section 10, pp. 45–46.

[3] Brand Blanshard, "The Case for Determinism", in Sidney Hook, ed., *Determinism and Freedom in the Age of Modern Science*, New York, 1961, p. 21.

[4] Blanshard uses 'constraints' and 'causes' interchangeably. See next quotation, which comes immediately before this one in his text.

of the previous party was, if you like, the cause of my refusing now. But it did not necessitate a refusal on my part. I could perfectly well have accepted—I might have decided it was my duty to put up with being bored for the sake of sociability. I had a reason for refusing, but my refusing was not inevitable, ineluctable, necessitated or determined.

Some philosophers, however, do use the word 'determined' in a wider sense, in which it is more or less equivalent to 'explained'. So far as ordinary usage goes, it is perfectly permissible: we do speak of a man's decision being "determined by the need to preserve his reputation". Blanshard instances a musician composing a piece or a logician making a deduction.[1] But although we use these locutions in common parlance, it only generates confusion to use them in philosophy. For the reasons which "determine" a composer to add a particular bar to his composition are parts of some sort of rational explanation, not a regularity one; they do not enable us to make predictions in advance, but only to see how right it was *ex post facto*. It is the mark of creative genius that it is original and unpredictable; although after it has manifested itself, its *rationale* is manifest also. There is no question of denying the artist's freedom, or of explaining away his stroke of genius as not being his but the inevitable result of circumstance. To explain his achievement is to explain it as *his*. Therefore it is not the sort of determinism with which we need to be concerned. The only relevance it has to the freedom of the will is that it provides one *route* whereby philosophers are led from possibly true and certainly innocuous premises to dangerously false and disastrous conclusions. It is easy to accept "determinism" in some dilute sense, in which all that is being claimed is that there is some reason for every action, and then believe that one is committed to determinism in a strong sense, in which all our actions are causally determined by conditions outside our control because occurring before our birth. Having agreed that there is a *rationale* to everything, we allow that each thing is rationally necessary—morally necessary, artistically necessary, aesthetically necessary—and then drop the adverb that qualifies the systematically ambiguous term 'necessary' and assume that they are all necessary, pure and simple, that is to say, physically necessary. But the shift is illegitimate. Our starting-point was the principle

[1] *Op. cit.*, pp. 26–30.

that every event has an explanation; which is not the same as, and does not imply, the contention that every event has a regularity explanation.

The shift from the wide, unspecified, sense of 'explanation' to the narrow causal one is made less glaring and more plausible in virtue of three considerations. First, there is a corresponding shift between *methodological* and *ontological* interpretations of the principle of universal causation. Second, the argument is often made to proceed through the negative concepts 'random' or 'chance'. Third, an explicit metaphysical doctrine that regularity explanations are the only real explanations is sometimes invoked. "Nothing," according to Leucippus,[1] "occurs by chance, but there is a reason and a necessity for everything."[2] He seems to be talking ontologically about the nature of things, how things are. But the appeal to reason is more methodological—how we are to think of the world, and how conduct our enquiries—in tone. Chrysippus[3] is more explicitly ontological. He says

Everything that happens is followed by something else which depends on it by causal necessity. Likewise, everything that happens is preceded by something with which it is causally connected. For nothing exists or has come into being in the cosmos without a cause. There is nothing in it that is completely divorced from all that went before. The Universe will be disrupted and disintegrate into pieces and cease to be a unity functioning as a single system, if any uncaused movement is introduced into it. Such a movement will be introduced, unless everything that exists and happens has a previous cause from which it of necessity follows. In their view, the lack of cause resembles a *creatio ex nihilo* and is just as possible.[4]

---

[1] fl. c. 440 B.C.

[2] οὐδὲν χρῆμα μάτην γίνεται, ἀλλὰ πάντα ἐκ λόγου τε καὶ ὑπ'ἀνάγκης in G. S. Kirk and J. E. Raven, *The Presocratic Philosophers*, Cambridge, 1957, no. 568; and in H. Diehls, *Fragmente der Vorsokratiker*, 6th ed. by W. Kranz, Berlin, 1951, 67B2; for a useful account see S. Sambursky, *The Physical World of the Greeks*, tr. Merton Dagut, London, 1956 and 1963, pp. 158–176.

[3] Lived c. 280–207 B.C.

[4] *Apud* Alexander of Aphrodisias *De Fato* 22; in J. von Arnim, *Stoicorum Veterum Fragmenta*, Leipzig, 1903, II, 945. παντί τε τῷ γενομένῳ ἕτερόν τι ἐπακολουθεῖν, ἠρτημένον ⟨ἐξ⟩ αὐτοῦ ἐξ ἀνάγκης ὡς αἰτίου, καὶ πᾶν τὸ γινόμενον ἔχειν τι πρὸ αὐτοῦ, ᾧ ὡς αἰτίῳ συνήρτηται. μηδὲν γὰρ ἀναιτίως μήτε εἶναι μήτε γίνεσθαι τῶν ἐν τῷ κόσμῳ διὰ τὸ μηδὲν εἶναι τῶν ἐν αὐτῷ ἀπολελυμένον τε καὶ κεχωρισμένον τῶν προγεγονότων ἁπάντων. διασπᾶσθαι γὰρ καὶ διαιρεῖσθαι καὶ μηκέτι

It would be unreasonable to criticize severely the confusion between ontological and methodological interpretations of the Principle of Universal Causation: indeed the distinction, as we shall see,[1] is a difficult one to sustain absolutely. We are all inclined to construe our fundamental principles as being ones about Reality. Many modern scientists would feel that Chrysippus expressed exactly what they felt. If pressed, we should allow that the principle that Every Event has a Cause may be taken as an ontological principle, about the nature of things; but then we should be very much on our guard against unconsciously supposing that since 'every event has a cause (*i.e.* an explanation)' is a statement about Reality, about the nature of things, therefore the cause must be a thingly cause (*i.e.* an explanation in terms of things, a regularity explanation). Subject to an important qualification,[2] I shall argue that we can say 'Every event has an explanation', and this is a statement about the universe. But the explanations are not all causal or regularity ones, and carry no determinist implications.

With the advent of quantum mechanics, the Leucippus fallacy has been revived, so that even if the human body is subject to quantum indeterminism, it still may be argued that it does not give the libertarian what he wants. Undetermined actions are random actions. But a man's random actions are not those we can usefully ask him his reasons for undertaking, or hold him responsible for. "A genuinely uncaused action could hardly be said to be an action of the agent at all;" says Nowell-Smith[3] "for in referring the action to an agent we are referring it to a cause." ". . . if one of our actions happened by 'pure chance' in the sense in which, according to modern physics, the change of state of a particular radium atom happens by pure chance, then this action would not be one for which we could be held *responsible*."[4]

τὸν κόσμον ἕνα μένειν, αἰεὶ κατὰ μίαν τάξιν τε καὶ οἰκονομίαν διοικούμενον, εἰ ἀναίτιός τις εἰσάγοιτο κίνησις. ἣν εἰσάγεσθαι, εἰ μὴ πάντα τὰ ὄντα τε καὶ γινόμενα ἔχοι τινα αἴτια προγεγονότα, οἷς ἐξ ἀνάγκης ἕπεται· ὅμοιόν τε εἶναί φασιν καὶ ὁμοίως ἀδύνατον τὸ ἀναιτίως τῷ γίνεσθαί τι ἐκ μὴ ὄντος. tr. S. Sambursky, *op. cit.*, p. 170.
[1] See below Section 30, pp. 168–170.   [2] See below, pp. 60–61.
[3] P. H. Nowell-Smith, "Freewill and Moral Responsibility", *Mind*, LVI, 1947, p. 47.
[4] J. J. C. Smart, "Free-Will, Praise and Blame", *Mind*, LXX, 1961, p. 296; compare Frederick Vivian, *Human Freedom and Responsibility*,

Professor Ayer has argued the point repeatedly[1]

For [the moralist] is anxious to show that men are capable of acting freely in order to infer that they can be morally responsible for what they do. But if it is a matter of pure chance that a man should act in one way rather than another, he may be free but he can hardly be responsible. And indeed when a man's actions seem to us quite unpredictable, when, as we say, there is no knowing what he will do, we do not look on him as a moral agent. We look upon him, rather, as a lunatic.

and then, again,[2]

Either it is an accident that I choose to act as I do or it is not. If it is an accident, then it is merely a matter of chance that I did not act otherwise; and if it is merely a matter of chance that I did not choose otherwise, it is surely irrational to hold me morally responsible for choosing as I did. But if it is not an accident that I choose to do one thing rather than another, then presumably there is some causal explanation of my choice: and in that case we are led back to determinism.

Professor Smart's argument is more like Chrysippus'.[3] He gives two definitions

D1. I shall state the view that there is "unbroken causal continuity" in the universe as follows. It is in principle possible to make a sufficiently precise determination of the state of a sufficiently wide region of the universe at time t_o, and sufficient laws of nature are in principle ascertainable to enable a superhuman calculator to be able to predict any event occurring within that region at an already given time t^1.

London, 1964, pp. 117–118. A. C. MacIntyre, "Determinism", *Mind*, LXVI, 1957, p. 30; M. C. Bradley, *Mind*, LXVIII, 1959, p. 522; John Plamenatz, "Responsibility, Blame and Punishment", in Peter Laslett and W. G. Runciman, eds., *Philosophy, Politics and Society*, 3rd series, Oxford, 1967, pp. 178–179.

[1] A. J. Ayer, "Freedom and Necessity", *Polemic*, 5, 1946, p. 38; reprinted in A. J. Ayer, *Philosophical Essays*, p. 275. Compare R. E. Hobart, "Free Will as Involving Determinism", *Mind*, XLIII, 1934, p. 5. For later versions of Ayer's argument see A. J. Ayer, *The Concept of a Person*, London, 1963, p. 254; for a general criticism, see C. A. Campbell. *On Selfhood and Godhood*, London, 1957, lecture IX, Section 10, pp. 175–176.

[2] *Op. cit., Polemic*, p. 39, *Philosophical Essays*, p. 275.

[3] J. J. C. Smart, "Free Will, Praise and Blame", *Mind*, LXX, 1961, pp. 293–298.

D2. I shall define the view that "pure chance" reigns to some extent within the universe as follows. There are some events that even a superhuman calculator could not predict, however precise his knowledge of however wide a region of the universe at some previous time.

Smart then claims that his opponent must allow that an agent is not morally responsible for an action that comes about by "pure chance".[1] Since the two definitions are jointly exhaustive, it follows that all actions for which we can be held responsible are determined. We can briefly represent his argument thus. All, or almost all, actions can be explained. Often the spectator can give one or two explanations, and the agent nearly always can give his reasons. On the few occasions where a person acts for apparently no reason at all, we stigmatize his action as random, and wonder whether it should really be called *his* action, or even *an action*. Certainly we do not want to say that all our moral actions are random, and therefore, Smart argues, they must be determined.

All these arguments turn on an equivocation in the use of the terms 'random' or 'uncaused', or the phrase 'by pure chance'. These concepts are *negative* concepts. 'Random' means *in*explicable. But since the concepts of explanation, cause and prediction are themselves equivocal, the concepts 'random', 'uncaused' and 'by pure chance' are so too. The randomness of quantum mechanics is opposed to *physical* explanation.[2] It says nothing about whether there is any *human* or *rational* explanation to be offered. An action not altogether caused by antecedent physical conditions is in one sense uncaused, but not in the same sense as an action uncaused by the agent, which therefore is really not an action of his at all. There is a simple fallacy implicit in describing actions as genuinely uncaused, absolutely random or occurring by pure chance; for uncausedness, randomness and chance, are not qualities, which are either present or absent, and if present are always the same. They are, instead, chameleon words, which take their colour from their context, and cannot be transferred from one context to another, and still carry the same significance. We can reconstruct Leucippus' argument thus

[1] p. 296.
[2] See below, Section 20, pp. 109–110. For a fuller discussion of randomness and explanation, see J. R. Lucas, *The Concept of Probability*, Oxford, 1970, ch. VII, pp. 112–118.

Everything has *an* explanation (λόγος)
∴ Nothing is inexplicable
∴ Nothing occurs at random (μάτην)[1]
∴ Nothing is inexplicable in Hempel's sense,

or

Nothing occurs for which there is no explanation
∴ Everything has a regularity explanation
∴ There is a (regularity) necessity for everything

and the fallacy is obvious.

The argument from explicability is usually a muddle. Occasionally, however, it is advanced respectably, on the explicit claim that all explanation must be, really, regularity explanation. Although, as we have seen in our discussion of Hempel's analysis of explanation,[2] we cannot say that explanations as we know them in ordinary life are all regularity explanations, it can be maintained as an explicit metaphysical thesis that they must be. Materialists believe it. They regard things as the fundamental entities, and therefore regard thing-like explanation as the fundamental category of explanation. They are wrong, as I hope to show, to believe in things rather than in persons, but they are respectably wrong. Equally respectable, although equally wrong, are those followers of Hume, who hold that all valid reasoning must be either deductive or inductive. If that were true, it would follow that explanations, other than purely formal ones, must be regularity explanations, and then the disjunction 'Either random or (causally) explicable' would be exhaustive, and the argument for determinism valid. But there is no reason to believe that all reputable non-tautological arguments are inductive, but rather the reverse. For if there were any such reason, we should ask whether it was itself deductive or inductive. If it was deductive, from premises that were entirely analytic, then it would be an argument about the meaning of the words 'valid' and 'cogent' 'reason' and 'argument'. It would be laying down how they were to be used. But such a *fiat* would commit the Naturalistic Fallacy. We could always go on to ask whether we ought to accept valid reasons or be guided by cogent arguments, and

---

[1] The Greek word has also the senses idly, fruitlessly, in vain; *i.e.* it is opposed to what is teleologically explicable as well as to what is causally explicable.   [2] Section 9.

whether we ought not to accept invalid ones or be guided by non-cogent ones. If on the other hand it was an inductive argument or was based on synthetic premisses, then it is vulnerable to counter-examples. Many arguments have been urged by many people which are not on the face of it either invalid or deductive or inductive. In order to establish the truth of the thesis, each *prima facie* counter-example must be examined and shown to fall, first appearances notwithstanding, into one of the three categories. But this is not done. The thesis is used as a legislative (or, more politely, regulative) principle, to rule out reasons and arguments as invalid, without benefit of trial. Therefore the arguments for the thesis are not inductive either. Either, then, there are no valid reasons for accepting it at all—in which case there are also no valid reasons for accepting its determinist consequences—or there are valid reasons. But if there are, since they are neither deductive nor inductive, but nonetheless are valid, the thesis is false. For there are then valid reasons that are neither deductive nor inductive: which is what was denied.[1] With this more generous notion of reasoning and reasons goes a more generous notion of explaining and explanations, and hence the possibility of actions being undetermined causally without their being altogether inexplicable and random.

We may argue more positively for construing 'explanation' generously. For only so can *every* thing be explained. It is a weakness of any metaphysical scheme which selects one type of explanation (*e.g.* a regularity explanation) as *the* fundamental type of explanation, that even a complete explanation of that type cannot explain everything. It is always possible, as every child knows, to ask a further 'Why?' at the end of every explanation. And even if we have expanded an explanation to be a complete explanation, it is still possible to put the whole explanation in question. Given a purely deductive explanation, we may ask why the rules of inference should be what they are, and when given a meta-logical justification, ask for a further justification of that: the tortoise can always out-query Achilles. Given a causal explanation we can ask two questions: why the laws of nature should be what they are; and why the initial conditions should

---

[1] Some philosophers have objected to this argument on the grounds of its being self-referential. But the objection loses its force in view of the considerations of Sections 25 and 26.

have been what they were: and the materialist has no answer. Many other events he, and not only he, must dismiss as co-incidences, concomitances of phenomena, fortunate perhaps, but entirely fortuitous. A chance meeting of a friend is a coincidence: although there is an explanation of each person's being in a particular place at a particular time, there is no explanation of the event under the description of the two friends meeting each other. The origin of life, under that description, is similarly inexplicable by the materialist. His complete explanation is a complete explanation only of events described in his terms. Completeness is secured in part by ruling awkward questions unaskable. If, *per contra*, we want always to be able to ask questions and not rule out any as being inherently unanswerable—I am not sure it is a reasonable request, but it seems to be what the principle of Universal Causation comes to, taken as a methodological prin-ciple[1]—then we cannot fix on any one pattern of explanation as being the paradigm. When we have completed one type of explanation we must be ready to switch to another type, in order to answer questions which still arise, but can no longer be answered on the lines of the original explanation. If there is always to be a 'because', the 'becauses' must be of all sorts of types. The wider the universality of our principle of universal explicability, the wider the range of possible explanations.

It is sometimes argued that every event must have a cause, because only so can we manipulate events. The argument fails; because, when it comes to other people, we neither think that we can, nor that we ought to be able to, manipulate them. All that the argument from manipulability shows is that things must be fairly reliable and persons sometimes reasonable. Life would be impossible, as Nowell-Smith argues,[2] if the fish I have just decided to eat "is liable to turn into a stone or to disintegrate in mid-air or to behave in any other utterly unpredictable manner". But to exclude this radical unpredictability is not to embrace complete inevitability. For practical purposes, we do not re-quire strongly quantified universal laws, that under certain condi-tions a specific event will absolutely always happen, but only weakly quantified universal laws, that the event will usually

[1] See below, Section 30, pp. 168–170.
[2] P. H. Nowell-Smith, "Freewill and Moral Responsibility", *Mind*, LVII, 1948, p. 47.

happen.[1] Indeed, so far as our actual knowledge of material objects goes, we reckon ourselves lucky when we can go even as far as that. So far as other people are concerned, it is enough that we can sometimes influence them, either by argument and reason, or by virtue of our having under our control some factor which would be for them a reason for acting in the way we wish. You want my car. You offer me money for it. Being offered money is a perfectly good reason for my selling you my car. But it does not make it inevitable that I should sell it. I am perfectly free not to.

The argument from manipulation does not support determinism. Indeed, it argues against it, and shows that the whole notion of cause does not imply the truth of determinism, but, on the contrary, presupposes its falsity. For the notion of cause is based not, as Hume thought, on our *observing* constant conjunctions of events, but on our being able *to make things happen*. I can, if I want to, bring about a certain result, and afterwards, if I do so, say "I did it", or, more grandly, "I caused it". I discover that I can achieve some of my ends only by accomplishing certain means first, whereupon the end ensues. Construing 'cause' as a transitive relation, I say "I caused the means and the means caused the end and that is how I caused the end". In this way we obtain the third-personal use of 'cause'. It is a back-formation from the first-personal use which is the primary one and gave the original sense. The conceptual environment in which 'I cause', 'I do' and 'I make things happen' flourish is our normal untutored one in which men are the initiators of chains of events and I can cause things without myself having been caused: and although the third personal use is now much the more extensive, it is unlikely that even the third-personal meaning would survive being transplanted into a conceptual environment in which the root meaning could not survive.

This turns out to be the case. Even when reformulated so as to fit the third-personal use only, the notion of cause still requires that of the freedom of the will. Constant conjunction by itself does not rule out the possibility of pre-arranged harmony or of both events being consequences of some third event rather than being directly related to each other. Two college clocks always chime, the one shortly after the other; it may be that they are

---

[1] Compare Jonathan Bennett, "The Status of Determinism", *British Journal for the Philosophy of Science*, XIV, 1963–4, pp. 106–119.

electrically connected, but other explanations are possible. The decisive test would be for the observer to introduce an arbitrary alteration in the earlier-chiming clock, and see whether this has any effect on the other. More generally, we discover causal relations not by merely observing passively but by experimenting as well. We have to be agents, not just spectators. And the reason is this: we believe that as free agents we can introduce an arbitrary disturbance into the universe and thus destroy any pre-arranged harmony: under the transformations that our arbitary interventions produce, only real regularities will be preserved, and coincidental and pre-arranged ones will be destroyed. This argument is valid if we really are free agents. Unless we are, the argument is invalid, because we still have not ruled out the possibility of the agent's intervention and the occurrence of the second event both being consequences of some earlier determining factor. We just do not know, supposing the determinist thesis is to be true, what are the causal antecedents of my "deciding" to introduce an "arbitrary" alteration in the universe. It might be that the only occasions on which an experimenter could or would do this were occasions in which the occurrences of the second event were already going to be disturbed. Thus in this case, as in others, man can only have a true view of the universe and the laws of nature by excepting himself from their sway, and considering himself over against the universe, not as part of it, but independent of it, and not subject to its laws.[1]

A second general argument against determinism stems not from intervention in natural phenomena but communication with other sentient beings.[2] Communication is not manipulation. When I tell somebody something, I am not making him believe it or do anything: I am giving him a reason which he is free to accept or reject. It is a presupposition of communication that each party believes the other to have been, or to be, able to act otherwise. A linguistic utterance is one which the speaker could have not uttered, and which the hearer believes he need not have uttered, and which is intended, and known to be intended, to be taken in a particular way, but to which the response is not, and is

[1] See also, Isaiah Berlin, *Historical Inevitability*, Oxford, 1954, pp. 32–33; reprinted in *Four Essays on Liberty*, Oxford, 1969, pp. 70–71.

[2] See more fully, Frederick J. Crosson and Kenneth M. Sayre, eds., *Philosophy and Cybernetics*, London, 1967, pp. 28–29.

not supposed to be, automatic. There are important differences between our responses to linguistic utterances and conditioned reflexes. Conversation is not a series of parade-ground commands.[1]

[1] Compare below, Section 17, pp. 88-89.

§12

TYPES OF DETERMINISM

FOUR sorts of determinism have at various times been put forward, and have been felt to threaten the freedom of the will and human responsibility, besides the historical determinism we have already touched upon.[1] They are: logical determinism, theological determinism, psychological determinism, and physical determinism. There are many variants of each type. They all, in different ways, satisfy the three conditions for being frightening. Different types of arguments are adduced in support of each type, and different counter-arguments are needed to rebut them.

Logical determinism maintains that the future is already fixed as unalterably as the past. It is already written in the book of destiny: it is already formed in the womb of the past. Various arguments are put forward for this, often turning on the timelessness of truth. The predictions are infallible, because logically necessary. They are based on factors already obtaining at present, and therefore exclude the possibility of a subsequent change of mind, and in some cases—long-range predictions—exclude the possibility of any factor under the agent's control being relevant. And the predictions are completely specific.

Theological determinism argues that since God is omniscient, He knows everything, the future included. Since He is God, His knowledge is infallible. Since He is a personal God, temporal epithets must be capable of being ascribed to Him, and in particular, we must say that what He knows, He knows now. Therefore, as with logical determinism, the possibility of change of mind is always excluded, and, in the long run, of any human contribution to the course of events. And divine knowledge is not only infallible, but perfect and completely specific.

Psychological determinism maintains that there are certain psychological laws, which we are beginning to discover, enabling us to predict, usually on the basis of his experiences in early

[1] Section 11, pp. 51–52.

infancy, how a man will respond to different situations throughout his later life. It is suggested that we should, one day, have as much confidence in the laws of psychology as we do in the laws of physics. The basis of the predictions is always intended to be limited so as to exclude the innocuous predictions we make every day. And the claim is that the predictions could be specific enough to constitute a real threat to freedom.

Physical determinism is based on there being physical laws of nature, many of which have actually been discovered, and of whose truth we can reasonably hope to be quite certain, together with the claim that all other features of the world are dependent on physical factors. Given a complete physical description of the world at any one time, we can calculate its complete physical description at any other time, and then given the complete physical description at that other time, we can calculate also what all its other, non-physical, features must be. Hence on the basis of the physical factors at one time, which because they are physical exclude all personal factors, we can, at one remove, calculate what a person's future actions must, infallibly, be. And so again we have a threat to freedom.

§13

LOGICAL DETERMINISM OR FATALISM

THE fallacies of fatalism have fascinated philosophers since Aristotle first discussed the sea-battle that was going to be fought tomorrow.[1] Ryle expresses the argument thus:

Whatever anyone does, whatever happens anywhere to anything, could not *not* be done or happen, if it was true beforehand that it was going to be done or was going to happen. So everything, including everything that we do, has been definitely booked from any earlier date you like to choose. Whatever is, was to be. So nothing that does occur could have been helped and nothing that has not actually been done could possibly have been done.[2]

Such arguments are unconvincing. For one thing, they equivocate on the meaning of the word 'true': for another, they trade on our taking a studiously indefinite reference to the future as having been a very definite and specific one *ex post facto*.

The word 'true' in ordinary speech has an operational import. If I say 'X is true', I vouch for the truth of X, I promise that X. It follows that I may be able to say 'X is true' at one time and not at another; and therefore we have the locutions 'X was true', 'X will be true', 'X came true'. In mathematical logic, however, we often are Platonists, and deal with timeless propositions which are timelessly true or timelessly false. For such timeless entities we may reasonably stipulate that the Law of the Excluded Middle shall hold, and that every proposition must be either true or false, in this timeless sense, even if we poor mortals do not know which. The common case in ordinary life where we cannot say either that X is true or that X is false, is not allowed to matter. We may not at present be able to say which is the case, but one or the other must, in fact, timelessly hold. The fatalist then argues about some future event, *e.g.* that you will recover from an attack of flu; and says that either this statement is true or it is

---

[1] *De Interpretatione*, Ch. 9.
[2] Gilbert Ryle, *Dilemmas*, Cambridge, 1954, Ch. II, p. 15.

false. But if it is true that you will recover, then there is no need for you to take medicine now, while if it is false that you will survive, then there is no point in taking medicine now: so, either way, you cannot alter the future, for it is already now true that it is going to be whatever it will be.

We can fault this argument in its use of 'true' in a timeless sense, in order to ensure that either X is true or X is false, followed by a use of 'true' in a temporal sense, in order to allow us to argue from the truth of X at a subsequent date to the equal truth of X at an earlier date, or from the falsity of X at a subsequent date to the equal falsity of X at an earlier date. We may say simply that if we use 'true' and 'false' as technical terms of timeless logic, then it may be that the Law of the Excluded Middle holds, but no argument from antecedent truth can hold, because any temporal ascription of truth is, for this concept of truth, meaningless. If, on the other hand, we use 'true' and 'false' in a temporal way—which is perfectly legitimate according to our ordinary use of the words—then we cannot assume that it must be now already either true that you will recover or false that you will recover.[1] The exact formulation of an adequate tense logic for future contingents is a difficult and disputed matter. But we are not obliged to accept the Law of the Excluded Middle for dated statements in the way that we are for the timeless propositions of traditional logic.

Even if we lay down that the Law of the Excluded Middle shall hold for statements about the future, we may still fault the inference from trivial tautology to iron necessity as turning on an illegitimate shift from the safely indefinite to the dangerously definite. Ryle faults fatalism on this score. The fallacy, he says, consists in the "idea of the eternal but unsupported pre-existence of truths in the future tense".[2] It is "intolerably vacuous". We do not know, and cannot in principle know, what the truth was, until the event in question has actually come true. Until you actually scratch your nose, we do not know *which* of the two propositions 'You will scratch your nose' and 'You will not scratch your nose' *was* true. We may, if the logician wants to talk that way, allow that truth is a timeless, or omnitemporal,

[1] See more fully, Richard M. Gale, *The Language of Time*, London, 1968, ch. VIII; or J. R. Lucas, "True", *Philosophy*, XLIV, 1969, pp. 180–181.   [2] Gilbert Ryle, *Dilemmas*, Cambridge, 1954, p. 17.

property of propositions, so that *some* proposition about your scratching your nose was true all along, long before you scratched it, long before you were born. But if we make that concession, we must insist that the 'some' is to be taken entirely indefinitely. It is not some, a particular, proposition—one that I could have cited had you asked me—which was true, but some in the sense of the existential quantifier, not-none, which was; in Latin, not *quaedam* but *nonnulla*—indeed, in this case, *nescioquae*. I am allowing to the logician that true propositions do not pop into existence as things happen: but I am denying that he has a logical privileged access to the labels on the propositions ahead of time. Much as the Intuitionists will not allow a mathematician to draw conclusions about a mathematical entity unless he can say which one it is, so we disallow the logician's attempt to draw conclusions from a proposition's having a truth-value unless he can say which truth-value it has. And this he cannot do.

Logical determinism fails through indefiniteness. The logician may be able to ascribe a truth-value to propositions before they have "come true" (*or* not), but he cannot ascribe a definite one. He is to be contrasted with the maker of an almanack, whose predictions are (or would be, if he were not Delphically cautious) quite definite, but altogether lack an assurance of (logically) necessary truth. The logician deals in propositions that must be true—but we do not know which they are: the almanack maker deals in propositions which are adequately definite—but we do not know whether they are true. The logical determinist wants to have it both ways. He wants to avoid definiteness in order to secure (logically) necessary truth: but having secured necessary truth wants to claim definiteness in order to have the future determined. But he cannot eat his definiteness and have it.

Some poetic and popular expositions of fatalism speak of a Book of Destiny. Thus, Omar Khayyám:

> And the first morning of creation wrote
> What the last dawn of reckoning shall read.[1]

[1] Rendered by Edward FitzGerald. Compare Robert Grave's translation (of a different stanza)

> What we shall be is written, and we are so.
> Heedless of God or Evil, pen, write on!
> By the first day all futures were decided;
> Which gives our griefs and pains irrelevancy.

If there really is a book, all written down already, then the case is altered. For then the predictions are definite. The pre-existence of truth in the future tense is supported. There is a book, literally and non-metaphorically, and some one might, literally and non-metaphorically, read it. But what warrant then is there for supposing the book to be necessarily true? Having stumbled on the book of doom, how should I distinguish it from Old Moore's Almanack? We no longer can argue that it must be true on purely logical grounds. It was because he did not show his hand that the logician was immune to refutation and could claim logically necessary truth. Once he has put his cards on the table and said something definite, he may be found to be wrong. Only by being careful to say, in effect, nothing, can one avoid running the risk of being wrong: as a Pope is rumoured to have said "If one is infallible, one has to be very, very careful what one says." But the logical determinist has no other claims to infallibility than logical necessity, that is, vacuity. The Book of Destiny needs some further argument to authenticate it, perhaps theological, perhaps metaphysical. But then it ceases to be logical determinism. Logical determinism depends on purely logical arguments. And these, however expressed, are patently fallacious.[1]

[1] I do not discuss the many papers that have been published since Ryle's, because they have, for the most part, not questioned the falsity of fatalism, but the exact point at which the fallacy was committed. This is of interest to logicians, but does not concern us here. Fatalism has, however, been argued for by Richard Taylor, *The Philosophical Review*, LXXI, 1962, pp. 56–66. See also Bruce Aune, "Fatalism and Professor Taylor", *ibid.*, pp. 512–519; Raziel Abelson, "Taylor's Fatal Fallacy", same journal, LXXII, 1963, pp. 93–96; Richard Taylor, "A Note on Fatalism", *ibid.*, pp. 497–499.

§14

THEOLOGICAL DETERMINISM:
OMNISCIENCE AND FOREKNOWLEDGE

THE chief theological argument for determinism is the argument from omniscience, although other arguments, from omnipotence and from grace are also invoked. "If God knows the future beforehand," Ambrose wrote to Origen, "and it must come to pass, prayer is vain."[1] The existence of God gives body, so to speak, to the arguments of fatalism and makes them no longer vacuous. If God knows now what I shall do, then there is something now already fixed, which cannot at a later date be surreptitiously altered in order to come into conformity with the facts. The cards are already on the table. We cannot, if we seriously believe in God, and ascribe to Him any sort of knowledge remotely like human knowledge, use any of the Rylean remedies that remove the sting from logical determinism.

Many thinkers have nevertheless been reluctant to accept the implications of theological determinism. For, however much a Christian may believe in the omniscience of God, he also is committed to the freedom of man. Many different devices have been adopted to preserve freedom and responsibility in the face of omniscience. It has been argued that God's foreknowing is not a *cause* of the predicted action's taking place, and that therefore God is not responsible, but man who does cause it.

> They, therefore, as to right belonged,
> So were created, nor can justly accuse
> Their Maker, or their making, or their fate,
> As if Predestination overruled
> Their will, disposed by absolute decree

---

[1] Origen, *De Oratore*, V, 6. εἰ προγνώστης ἐστὶν ὁ Θεὸς τῶν μελλόντων, καὶ δεῖ αὐτὰ γίνεσθαι, ματαία ἡ προσευχή. tr. J. E. L. Oulton and Henry Chadwick, *The Library of Christian Classics*, Vol II, *Alexandrian Christianity*, London, 1954, p. 250.

Or high foreknowledge; they themselves decreed
Their own revolt, not I: if I foreknew,
Foreknowledge had no influence on their fault,
Which had no less proved certain unforeknown.[1]

Modal logic has been called in aid to distinguish conditional from unconditional necessities. The conditional proposition, 'if p then q', may be necessary without its following that the simple proposition, p, is necessary too. In symbols

$$\Box(p \supset q) \text{ does not entail } \Box q$$

Hence, it is argued, it does not follow that I must of necessity act in a particular way, $\Box q$, from the fact that the proposition 'if God foreknows that I am going to act in a particular way, then I must so act' is itself a necessary one, $\Box(p \supset q)$. The entailment holds only if we have the further proposition $\Box p$—that God necessarily foreknows that I am going to act in a particular way. And this premiss may be denied us: it is claimed that all we can assert is the simple indicative 'God foreknows that I am going to act in a particular way' and not the modal 'God necessarily foreknows... or 'God must foreknow...': for who are we to lay down necessities for God? And once this premiss is thus weakened, the entire argument for determinism collapses. For whereas

$$\Box p \supset \Box(p \supset q) \supset \Box q$$

is a theorem of modal logic,

$$p \supset \Box(p \supset q) \supset \Box q$$

[1] J. Milton, Paradise Lost, III, ll. 111–119; my italics. Compare Boethius, *De Consolatione Philosophiae*, V, iii, ll. 42ff., *Nam etiam si idcirco quoniam futura sunt, providentur, non vero ideo quoniam providentur eveniunt.* V, iv, ll. 13ff., *[ratio] quae quia praescientiam non esse futuris rebus causam necessitatis existimat, nihil impediri praescientia arbitrii libertatem putat.* Boethius was not the first, although in the West the best known, to argue thus. See Origen, *De Oratore*, VI, 3, οὐχὶ τῆς προγνώσεως τοῦ Θεοῦ αἰτίας γινομένης τοῖς ἐσομένοις πᾶσι, καὶ ἐκ τοῦ ἐφ᾽ἡμῖν τὴν ὁρμὴν ἡμῶν ἐνεργηθησομένοις, tr. J. E. L. Oulton and Henry Chadwick, *op. cit.*, p. 252. "But the foreknowledge of God is not the cause of all future events or of future action performed of us of our free will and mere motion." A few lines later Origen has an interesting anticipation of Leibniz's doctrine of the Pre-established Harmony "From foreknowledge, however, it follows that each act of free will is adapted to such an arrangement of the whole as the settled order of the universe demands". But see his *De Principiis* III, i, esp. 12, 13, 17 and III, ii, 4, which is much less determinist in tone. English translation by G. W. Butterworth, London, 1936, pp. 179, 182, 191, 217–218.

is not. Such a solution was much canvassed in the Middle Ages. Chaucer interrupts his Nun's Priest's Tale of Chauntecleer and Pertelote to observe

Witnes of hym that ony clerk is
That in scole is gret altercacioun
In this mater, and greet disputacion,
And hath ben of an hundrid thousand men.
But I ne can not bulte out the bren
As can the holy doctour Austyn,
Or Boece, or the bisshop Bradwardyn,
Whethir that goddis afore wetynge
Streynyth me needeles for to do a thing,—
"Nedly" clepe I simpyl necessite;
Or yf the fre choys be grauntyd me
To do that same thing, or do it nought,
Though god forwoot it or it was wroght;
Or yf his witynge streyneth nevyr a deel
But by necessite condicionel.[1]

Leibniz later argued likewise[2]; and so have many others.

It has also been argued that God is outside time, so that His foreknowledge of what we are going to do is not to be dated to any particular time, and *a fortiori* not to some time before the actions in question.[3] Again, it has been argued that what constitutes a person's being the person he is, are the situations and circumstances of his life; so that he could not demand not to do what he was going to do, without demanding to be a different person from the one he was.[4]

---

[1] *Canterbury Tales*,*4426–*4440; in World Classics ed. (Oxford), p. 259; spelling as in M.S. in Merton College Library.

[2] *Theodicy*, § 36, *Causa Dei*, § 43, *Fifth Letter to Clarke*, § 4 ff.

[3] Boethius, *De Consolatione Philosophiae*, V, vi, ll. 5ff.; esp. ll. 63ff. *scientia quoque eius omnem temporis supergressa motionem in suae manet simplicitate praesentiae infinitaque praeteriti ac futuri spatia complectens omnia quasi iam gerantur in sua simplici cognitione considerat. Itaque si praesentiam pensare velis qua cuncta dinoscit, non esse praescientiam quasi futuri sed scientiam numquam deficientis instantiae rectius aestimabis.* The same view is held by G. D. Yarnold, *The Moving Image*, London, 1966, esp. pp. 148–151 and 185–186. Samuel Clarke, *Sermons*, 7th ed., London, 1749, vol. I, p. 50, had protested, I think rightly, that it is, taken literally, an unintelligible way of speaking. See further my forthcoming *Treatise on Time and Space*.   [4] Leibniz, *Discourse on Metaphysics*, chs. XXX, XXXI.

These arguments do not convince. While it is true that to predict is not to cause, so that God could predict our actions without
necessarily causing them, nevertheless to predict a man's action
infallibly,[1] perhaps a long time before he was born, would be
incompatible with his being responsible for them. Nor can the
argument from modal logic ease the difficulty. It seems to work
only because the modality it expresses is a logical, not a temporal
one. If we take time seriously, we must believe that what is past—
including the fact that at some date in the past God foreknew
what I am going to do—is unalterable, and in that sense necessary; and then the modal argument is valid, $\Box q$ does follow, and
it is necessary that I shall act in a particular way.[2] The suggestion
that God is outside time is difficult to discuss, because its meaning
is unclear. There are no doubt many ways in which God is not
subject to temporal limitations as we human beings are. But if to
be outside time is to exclude God from all temporal experience—
as it must if it is to avoid the argument from foreknowledge—then
it is to deny God anything that could be called personality. We

[1] Compare Boethius, *De Consolatione Philosophiae*, V, iii, ll. 66ff.,
*Quonam modo deus haec incerta futura praenoscit? Nam si inevitabiliter
eventura censet quae etiam non evenire possibile est, fallitur; quod . . . sentire
nefas est. . . .*

[2] See the admirable discussion by Nelson Pike, "Divine Omniscience
and Voluntary Action", *Philosophical Review*, LXXIV, 1965, pp. 27–46.
John Turk Saunders, "Of God and Freedom", *Philosophical Review*,
LXXV, 1966, pp. 219–225, criticizes the conclusion, and draws a parallel
between God's knowing yesterday what I shall do today, and its being
true of Caesar's assassination that it occurred 2009 years before Saunders
wrote his paper. The latter, although a fact about Caesar, does not have
any determinist implications, because it asserts a relation; and a relation
depends on both the things it is a relation between; so that the temporal
relation between Caesar's assassination and Saunders writing his paper
depends on the latter as much as the former. But knowledge is not a
relation like that. To say that God knows what I am going to do is to say
that God could at some previous date say, in definite words, what I am
going to do. Knowledge is nothing if not definite. The cards are already
shown, at least to God. Therefore God's knowledge cannot depend on
what is yet to happen. And the problem remains. See further Nelson Pike,
"Of God and Freedom: A Rejoinder", *Philosophical Review*, LXXV,
1966, pp. 369–379. For a logical parallel to Saunders' criticism, see A. N.
Prior, *Past, Present, and Future*, Oxford, 1967, Ch. VII, Sections 3–4, pp.
121–127; and "The Formalities of Omniscience", *Philosophy*, XXXVII,
1962, pp. 114–129; reprinted in A. N. Prior, *Papers on Time and Tense*,
Oxford, 1968, pp. 26–44.

could properly say that Plato's Form of the Good was outside time, and use the statement to resist any temporal paradoxes that an ingenious opponent might extract from the Form of the Good being the principle of all things. But to be a person one must be capable of consciousness, and all consciousness is temporal. Time is a *distentio animi*, as St. Augustine said.[1] Therefore God, if He is a personal God must have temporal experience, and we can ask of His knowledge not only what He knows, but what He knows now. And then the argument from foreknowledge is under way.

The real solution is to the problem of God's omniscience is to be found by drawing a parallel with His omnipotence. Although God is able to do all things, we do not think He does do all things. Not only do we often ascribe events to human agencies or natural causes rather than to divine action, but we allow that some things happen against God's will. Although He could intervene to prevent the plans of the wicked from coming to fruition, often He does not. And the reason commonly given by theologians is that God often refrains from intervening in the world in order to preserve man's freedom of choice. He allows man to be independent and to make real choices which are really effective, in spite of the fact that they are often not the choices that God would have had us make, and in spite of the fact that they will often involve other men in undeserved suffering. But if God is prepared to compromise His omnipotence for the sake of human freedom, surely then He would be prepared to compromise His omniscience also. If He suffers His will to be confined, in order that His creatures may have room to make their own decisions, He must allow His understanding to be abridged, in order to allow men privacy to form their own plans for themselves.

It seems to me entirely unobjectionable that God should limit His infallible knowledge as He does His power, in order to let us be independent of Him. Such a self-limitation would not be open to Leibniz's objection that it would make God "like the God of the Socinians, who lives only from day to day."[2] For it limits only His *infallible* knowledge. God could still know us and predict our actions in the way our friends do, without its constituting

---

[1] *Confessions*, Book XI, ch. XXVI, 33.
[2] Second letter to Clarke, Section 9, ed. H. G. Alexander, *Leibniz–Clarke correspondence*, Manchester, 1956, p. 19. See also Clarke's *Boyle Lectures*.

any threat to freedom. The Christian religion, with its emphasis on the humanity of God, must ascribe to Him all human modes of knowledge, as well as the more absolute ones of theism generally. Fallible foreknowledge is enough to enable God not to live only from day to day, but to foresee the likely course of events and to take such actions, consistent with human freedom, as will work out for the best in the context of those decisions men are likely to take.[1]

Two other arguments are given for determinism on theological grounds: the theocentric *nisus* of theologians leads them to use the theological superlative too freely, and to ascribe not only all honour and glory but all power and dominion to the Almighty; and the sinner's sense of his own failure and futility finds expression in the doctrine of the total depravity of the human race, that we have absolutely no power of ourselves to help ourselves. Confusion about the logical geography of the concept of grace has often supported both lines of argument. Theologians are insufficiently reluctant to contradict themselves, and have often taken unwholesome delight in invoking human freedom to explain away evil, and denying it in order to attribute all good to God. The most theocentric of all the fathers was St. Augustine; and it was he who formed the mind of Western Christendom. Although he explicitly stated that man does have free will, and wrote a book under that title,[2] the whole tendency of his mind was to attribute everything to God, and in his later life, in controverting Pelagius, he came to hold a position in which human freedom has no part to play. Calvin but followed where St.

---

[1] The reader should be warned that the author is an Anglican, and that these views are contrary to the formularies both of Rome and of Geneva. See, *e.g.*, *Concilium Valentinum de praedestinatione*, Can. 2 and *Concilium Vaticanum*, Sessio III, Cap. I, "Omnia enim nuda et aperta sunt oculis ejus, ea etiamquae libera creaturarum actione futura sunt" (quoted by A. G. N. Flew, in *New Essays in Philosophical Theology*, London, 1955, p. 151); Calvin, *Articles Concerning Predestination*, tr. J. K. S. Reid, *Library of Christian Classics*, vol. XXII, *Calvin: Theological Treatises*, London, 1954, pp. 179–180. For a fuller discussion of the problems raised by Omniscience, see Charles Harteshorne, *Man's Vision of God*, New York, 1941, ch. 3, pp. 98–105, and 139–140.

[2] *De Libero Arbitrio*, tr. John H. S. Burleigh, in *The Library of Christian Classics*, vol. VI, *Augustine: Earlier Writings*, London, 1953.

Augustine led, and much of the determinism of the modern mind may be attributed to its Reformed upbringing.

Some of these arguments are purely theological, and need to be answered in purely theological terms—their God is an unchristian God and their man is not a human being, and however impeccable their logic, their religion is not Christianity: others have been transposed into secular terms, and are felt now as arguments not so much for theological, as for psychological, or for physical, determinism, and are better discussed under those heads.

§15

PSYCHOLOGICAL DETERMINISM

PSYCHOLOGICAL determinism is an aspiration rather than a threat. It needs exposing rather than arguing against. We know of no psychological laws which enable us to make anything more than very tentative predictions of extreme vagueness. Psychological determinism has drawn popular support from the fact that some disturbances in adult life have been explained more or less convincingly as the result of experiences in early infancy. But the explanations offered by the psychoanalysts are seldom of the Hempelian regularity kind.[1] The very fact that they are convincing stems from their giving the human *rationale* of the symptoms rather than being a bare statement of a covering law discovered to be invariably true. Non-Hempelian explanations do not convert into predictions in the easy way that Hempelian ones do. In so far as we can construct a prediction from an explanation in human terms, it will be a guarded or fallible prediction like all other human predictions. We may believe that if we spare the rod we shall spoil the child, or that if we punish him for bed-wetting we shall jeopardise his chances of sexual satisfaction in married life. But these are not cast-iron predictions. It remains possible that an unbeaten child will nevertheless not be spoilt, or a punished bed-wetter achieve a sexually satisfactory marriage. We may be sure enough of our predictions to act on them, but not so sure as to deny the possibility of human freedom.

Moreover, such predictions as psychologists do make, are in very general terms. They do not predict, or pretend to be able to predict, that at 10 a.m. on March 25 of next year I shall assume such and such a bodily posture, and utter such and such words. Rather, they predict that I shall have a tendency towards anxiety-neurosis, I shall be over-scrupulous in the keeping of promises, and I shall have an obsessive horror of dirt. These are dispositions or tendencies. They do not determine actions. Only by an ex-

[1] See above Section 9.

trapolation of breath-taking audacity could we come to believe that so many of a man's dispositions were predictable that his response to every situation was predictable too. Not only should we have to make the perilous, though possible, assumption that psychology would become as mathematical a discipline as physics, in which pain or fear could be measured as precisely as temperature or current, but we should have to assume that human beings are only finitely complex, and, what we know to be false, that they are unaffected by repetition.

Causal laws and functional dependences are formulated with only a finite number of variables. Else they could not be formulated at all, and even if they could would be in danger of being vacuous.[1] They therefore apply only to situations which can be specified in all relevant respects by a finite number of characteristics. But we cannot condense the infinite variety of a human being or a human situation into a finite list of characteristics. In physics we can secure finitude by deeming many factors to be irrelevant: but with men we cannot be sure before the event that any factor is irrelevant, if only because men have minds and can make any factor relevant simply by so regarding it. This apart, our experience of human personality is one of infinitude.[2] If, therefore, we are basing our argument on our experience of what human beings are like, we cannot claim to be able to analyse them into only a finite number of relevant features, or that causal laws formulated in terms of only a finite number of variables will be applicable.

Moreover, each human being is not only infinitely complex, but unique. The same is true of situations, not only because of the uniqueness of the persons involved but additionally because each man remembers his own experiences and has heard tell of other people's. I can take a body of gas round the Carnot cycle as often as I have a mind to, but each time I repeat an experiment with a human subject he will become either better or more bored. Even if human affairs were not infinitely complex, we should still be unable to obtain a sufficient number of similar instances on which to base our predictions. Those who deny that Hannibal and Rome were each unique have difficulty nonetheless in producing

[1] See below, Section 17, p. 90.
[2] See further J. D. Mabbott, *An Introduction to Ethics*, London, 1966, pp. 114–115, and the quotations given there.

an adequate number of Hannibaline men marching on Romish cities to verify the alleged law that in such cases the man always takes the city. Similarly the psychologist, even if he thinks he can specify all the relevant factors in a situation, so that a universal law could be formulated, will find it very hard to produce instances to justify his claim that the law must hold without exception. Freud's case-histories are often convincing: it is only when he starts formulating psychological laws that he becomes ridiculous.

Only by extreme extrapolation can we suppose that psychology will change so radically that it will come to predict with a fair degree of certainty a man's response to every situation. Why do people make such an extrapolation? There seems to be three reasons: people are unclear what psychology is; they are confused by the logical form of certain types of psychological explanation; and they are paying unconscious tribute to some thesis of physicalism.

The word 'psychology' has no fixed definition. It ranges from the purely physiological enquiries of those who study rats to the insights of novelists and playwrights. In the former sense psychological research could conceivably yield Hempelian predictions that were infallible and were based on factors outside the agent's control. In the latter sense, it yields something like "rational" explanations, and we may reasonably think that all our actions can be explained in this sense: but such explanations are not equivalent to infallible predictions based on factors outside the agent's control. A person of great psychological insight may be able to explain our actions to us, and we may feel that all our actions are susceptible of some sort of explanation. But that is not to say that they were predictable or are determined. Only if they are all based entirely on factors outside our control, and have the same degree of invariable validity as laws of physics, can they support determinism. But psychological laws of that sort are psychological in a different sense of the word 'psychology', and there is no reason to suppose that all (or anything like all) our actions are subject to psychological laws in that sense.

One sort of explanation which we sometimes call psychological is where we explain actions in terms of motives. 'Why did she say that?' we ask, and are told 'She is very jealous.' We find it very illuminating to explain actions in terms of jealousy, ambition, gratitude and the like. But we often fail to realise that these explanations are unlike explanations in terms of antecedent circumstances. Although often there are antecedent circumstances in virtue of which the explanation is appropriate, the explanations themselves are *re-describing* explanations rather than causal ones. In saying that she is jealous we are describing the *sort* of things she does and says. An ambitious man is one who characteristically never lets slip an opportunity of self-advancement, and always is working away to further his career.[1] We explain the girl's words or the man's deeds by re-describing them as the sort of thing the girl says or the man does. It is often explanatory, but it is an explanation in terms of a diagnosis, not a recipe, a formal cause, in Aristotle's terminology, not an efficient one.

There is nothing wrong with such explanations, but they can be misunderstood. In particular, we can easily be misled into arguing in a circle. We explain a person's action by saying it is the sort of thing he does do: but the evidence for his being disposed to do that sort of thing is his actually on occasion so acting. If a man fails to do the generous thing, then it counts against his being a generous man: and so, by contraposition, if he is a generous man, he must, logically must, sometimes act generously. And thus when we explain a particular action of generosity, it seems that the man could not but have done the action in question. The action is evidence for the disposition: but the disposition logically necessitates the action. Therefore every action is necessitated.[2]

Few arguments are so patently circular as I have made out. The issues are confused in practice, because most motives are not purely dispositional[3] but (like jealousy) are mental predicates too. Moreover, dispositions are concerned not with one action only, but a whole run of them. The jealous girl and the ambitious man have normally manifested their jealousy or ambition on previous occasions, so that the action in question is not the only evidence

[1] Compare Ryle's account of vanity in *The Concept of Mind*, London, 1949, pp. 86–87, 171–172.
[2] Compare, for example, Jonathan Edwards in Paul Ramsey, ed., *Freedom of the Will*, New Haven, 1957, p. 148, pp. 225–226.
[3] For much fuller discussion, see Phillipa Foot, "Free Will as involving Determinism", *Philosophical Review*, 66, 1957, pp. 445–447.

we have to go on. These complexities make it easier to argue in a circle without realising it. If we ask the vaguer question, whether a man can act out of character, we are easily impelled to the conclusion that he cannot, arguing that if he has such and such a character, then he must have acted in the appropriate way, and that he must have such and such a character because he did act in the appropriate way. Such logical necessities are too strong for us to be able to break them: but, properly regarded, are seen to be too thin for us to need to be worried by them.

St. Augustine, followed by Kant and, in recent years C. A. Campbell and W. G. Maclagan,[1] proposed a sort of partial psychological determinism based on a confusion between the different senses of 'psychological'. We are only free, on this view, when we act morally. For if we do not act morally, there must be some other psychological (in Kant "pathological") explanation of our actions; in which case we were not free to do anything else. We do whatever we do either for some moral reason which we have autonomously willed to do or because it is what we want to do, what we most desired to do. But if it was what we most desired to do, then—unless we escape from our desires by making a moral choice—our action is determined by our desires. But it is a different sense of 'determined'. In spite of the high standing of those who put it forward, the argument is invalid; although the sense of liberation which a moral man experiences when he makes an autonomous choice is of great importance in moral philosophy.

Many psychologists are physicalists. They believe that

---

[1] St. Augustine, *De Libero Arbitrio*, bk. I, vii, 16–xvi, 35; esp. xv, 32–xvi, 35. Kant, *Groundwork of the Metaphysic of Morals*, ch. III, p. 98 (tr. H. J. Paton, *The Moral Law*, London, 1948, p. 114); but see Paton's footnote and *Critique of Judgement*, Section 87n. (tr. J. C. Meredith, Oxford, 1952, pp. 116–117). C. A. Campbell, *Scepticism and Construction*, London, 1931, chs. 4–5; C. A. Campbell, "Is 'Freewill' a Pseudo-problem?", *Mind*, LX, 1951, pp. 441–465, esp. pp. 460–464; W. G. Maclagan, "Freedom of the Will", *Proceedings of the Aristotelian Society*, Supplementary Volume, XXV, 1951; C. A. Campbell, "Self-Activity and its Modes", *Contemporary British Philosophy*, 3rd series, ed. H. D. Lewis, London, 1956, esp. pp. 106–114; but see further, C. A. Campbell, *On Selfhood and Godhood*, London, 1957, lecture ix, Section 4. R. L. Franklin, "Moral Libertarianism", *Philosophical Quarterly*, 12, 1962, pp. 24–35. C. A. Campbell, "Moral Libertarianism: a reply to Mr. Franklin", *Philosophical Quarterly*, 12, 1962, pp. 337–347.

psychological laws can be reduced to physiological ones, which can, in turn, be reduced to chemical, and ultimately to physical, ones. Physicalism gives them warrant for ascribing to psychological laws, when discovered and properly formulated, the same degree of certainty as we ascribe to the laws of physics, and enables them to feel that the laws of psychology are really infallible, in spite of all the evidence to the contrary. It is a metaphysical doctrine. It has to be argued for on other than psychological grounds, and what it establishes, if true, is not psychological determinism, but physical determinism. And therefore we consider it under that heading.

PHYSICAL DETERMINISM

PHYSICAL Determinism is easily the most important type of determinism today. It is the only one that poses a credible threat to freedom. None of the other sorts of determinism are convincing, even though it may be a little tricky to put one's finger precisely on the mistake. But physical determinism is frightening. The arguments for it are forceful. The world-view suggested by physics is strongly supported by the success of the physical sciences in explaining phenomena, and even if it has to be amended in some detail, it remains both well supported and incompatible with freedom. We therefore need to examine it with great care.

Historically, physical determinism arose from a marriage of Newton's physics and Locke's metaphysics. The universe was conceived as being really composed of point-particles, permanent, impenetrable and possessing mass, all qualitatively identical except for differences in position and velocity. The motions of these particles could be completely described by Newtonian mechanics, which was a deterministic theory. The state—*i.e.* the positions and velocities of all the particles—at any one moment was determined by the state at any other moment. Given complete information about a system at any one time, its state at any other time was determined: that is, the proposition expressing the state of the system at the other time was a logical consequence of the conjunction of the proposition expressing the system at the one time and the postulates of Newtonian mechanics. This represented what the universe was really like. Although to the unenlightened eye it might seem to be composed of sticks and stones which only very imperfectly obeyed Newton's laws and were subject to many changes which were not obviously changes of velocity or position, we should, if we had microscopic eyes, be able to see the primary substances with their primary qualities. The determinist implications ensued provided only that the following conditions were satisfied: there was one all-embracing scientific calculus or language into which all relevant statements about the world in other languages could be translated: causal laws (or functional dependences) could be formulated in this language: and these causal laws were complete and deterministic.

Any scientific theory offers correlations between state-descriptions: that is, a scientific theory picks out certain characteristics of a substance or a situation or system and says that these are connected in some specified way. Thus, at a very simple level, we may say that a metal which is yellow and ductile and not attacked by nitric acid, will melt at 1,068°C, boil at 2,200°C, and be dissolved by a mixture of nitric and hydrochloric acids, and will have a specific gravity of 19·3. More complicated, we have Ohm's law, that the current flowing through a conductor is proportional to the voltage and inversely proportional to the resistance; or again, Charles' gas law, that for a unit mass of gas, $PV = RT$, where P is the pressure, V the volume, T the absolute temperature and R a constant: and there are other, far more complicated, laws which chemists and physicists believe to be true. In each case there is a state-description, which picks out the characteristics of the substance or situation or system the law is concerned with: in our first example, whether the substance in question is a metal, its colour and ductility, its melting point, its specific gravity and two of its chemical properties: in the second example, three electrical properties of a conductor: in the third, temperature, pressure and volume of a body of gas. The force of the law is then to say that not all state-descriptions are equally possible, but the possible combinations of factors that go to make up a state-description are restricted in some sort of way. Thus, in being given the characteristic properties of gold we are being told that no substance can be a yellow ductile metal attacked by a mixture of nitric and hydrochloric acids but not by nitric acid and yet not have a melting point of 1,068°C nor have a specific gravity of 19·3. Likewise, the effect of Ohm's law is to rule out the possibility of systems in which say, a voltage of 100 volts is applied across a simple resistance of 10 ohms and a current of 50 (or any other value than 10) ampères flows. Equally with the gas law, we know that not every combination of temperature, pressure and volume is possible, but, in this case, for given values of the temperature and pressure one and only one value of the volume is possible.

In order that deterministic conclusions should follow, two further conditions are necessary: it is necessary that the state-description should be in some sense complete, and it is necessary that the time variable should so enter into the laws that, together with a state-description of the system at some earlier time, the state-description of the system at a later time can be deduced. The latter requirement is met by Newtonian mechanics. Indeed, Newton's laws of motion enable us to work out from a state-description of a system at a given time its state-descriptions not only at all subsequent times, but at all preceding times too. Newtonian mechanics, however, is by itself not enough to establish determinism: we could believe that the stars in their courses were guided by Newtonian laws, and that the same explanations would hold good on earth for the flight of ping-pong balls, billiard balls, flies on frictionless bicycle wheels, and falling apples; and yet hold that human beings, who were neither stars nor terrestrial point-particles, were still free to choose between one course of action and another.[1] Newtonian mechanics by itself would not have been enough to establish scientific determinism: what was needed, and was effective, was the conjunction of Newton's physics with Locke's metaphysics.

Locke's doctrines of substance and of primary and secondary qualities together did the job of ensuring that the state-descriptions of the universe with which Newtonian mechanics dealt were in some important sense complete. For Newton, a system is completely described in mechanical terms if the position and momentum of every point-particle was given. Locke maintained that all other characteristics—notably colour and sound—could be explained in terms of the configuration and motions, *i.e.* positions and momenta, of the point-particles that constituted the substances. This additional doctrine makes Newtonian mechanics lead to determinist conclusions. Without it, mechanics differs nothing from thermodynamics. Each theory determines some but not all aspects of systems: mechanics would determine the mechanical behaviour of unimpeded particles, but not their colour or their sounds; and, in as much as human beings are not particles, it would not give an explanation of their own activities: fire a man from a catapult, and Newton's laws will describe his trajectory; but a man walking round his garden or writing a book is not what

[1] See above, Section 7, p. 32.

Newton's mechanics by itself deals with. Only when we add Locke's doctrine that all substances are fundamentally particulate in nature, and that *every* characteristic of macroscopic objects can be accounted for in terms of the positions and momenta of the fundamental particles, do we have determinist conclusions. For then we can translate, or better, represent, *every* characteristic of the world in terms of *mechanical* state-descriptions; and therefore we can give a *complete* description of the world by giving a mechanical state-description (*i.e.* giving the positions and momenta) of the fundamental particles. According to Locke, if we know the positions and momenta of the fundamental particles, then we should, if we knew enough science and were clever enough, know everything, in every respect. And therefore the future is determined, because the fundamental particles obey Newtonian laws, and therefore their positions and momenta are determined for all future times, and their positions and momenta at any future time determine everything else at that time. So the future state of the universe, in *every* respect, not just some respects only, is determined.

We can now see that determinism needs two theses to establish it. One is that there is some special way of talking about the world, such that every statement describing the world can be represented in this way of talking, *i.e.* such that a state-description in this way of talking is a *complete* description of the world. The other is that there is a determinist theory formulated in the special way of talking and correlating every sort of variable that occurs in it, so that from the state-description at any one time we can, or could if we knew the laws, calculate the state-description at any future time. Locke's theory of substance and of primary and secondary qualities and Newton's laws of motion and of universal gravitation fulfil these requirements, but they are not the only possible ones. We need not see the world as made up of atoms obeying Newtonian laws in order to be determinists: we could equally believe that all phenomena could be accounted for in terms of electro-magnetic fields and that these conformed to determinist laws, or we could retain our atomism but believe that the fundamental particles of which the universe was ultimately composed obeyed non-Newtonian, but still determinist, laws.

There are many objections to physical determinism. Human beings are not physical systems within the meaning of the Act.

Physical systems are isolated from other influences, whereas human beings, like all biological organisms, are in perpetual interplay with their environment. They are constantly taking in and discarding material substances in their metabolic processes, with corresponding dissipation or absorption of energy. With sentient beings, the external influences acting on them may extend to the remotest parts of the universe.[1] But the physical determinist is not impressed. He is prepared to extend the physical system under consideration to include the whole universe if necessary, in spite of objections that the whole universe cannot be an isolated system because there is nothing it is isolated from. More reasonably, the influence of remote parts of the universe can properly be discounted in most cases. So long as the stars continue in their courses, their influence on sublunary affairs is limited, constant and calculable, and they will fight neither for nor against any mortal man's affairs.[2]

Some philosophers say flatly that human beings are totally different from machines, and that there is nothing further to be said. Our responses are notably unmachinelike. The wooden Wodens in Wagner's operas gain some of their effect by behaving like machines, not men: and military commanders devote much time and effort to drilling their men to suppress their human responses and acquire those of an automaton. More particularly, since human beings are capable of rational behaviour, and rational explanations are different from regularity explanations, it is implausible to expect the behaviour of a machine to simulate that of a man in his rational moods. Rational arguments, unlike regularity explanations, are "dialectical" in form.[3] There is always room for a further 'but'. There always may be some further argument which will invalidate the justification or explanation offered, and this argument may not be any further fact about the physical world or factor of the situation. When we are invoking moral justifications or rational explanations, therefore, the logic of the discourse requires us to keep open the possibility of the same situation demanding some different action or the same facts supporting some different belief. But a complete

[1] See below, Section 20, p. 111.
[2] See J. R. Lucas, "Causation", in *Analytical Philosophy*, 1st series, ed. R. J. Butler, Oxford, 1962, pp. 57–58.
[3] See above, Section 9, pp. 42–43; Section 10, pp. 49–50.

regularity explanation—which is in principle available for the output of a machine or the development of a physical system—rules out this possibility. Moral commitment is essentially vulnerable: truth is a perpetual possibility of being wrong. And therefore we cannot hope to explain these completely by any regularity explanation.[1] But again the physical determinist is not impressed. His is a metaphysical position for which he can adduce powerful arguments, and he is prepared to ride rough-shod over difficulties, always believing that he will one day be able to account within his own scheme for any phenomena which seem at present to count against it. We need to make the arguments on both sides much more exact if we are to be able to reach a decisive conclusion.

[1] See further below, Section 21; and J. R. Lucas, "True", *Philosophy*, XLIV, 1969, pp. 175–186.

§17

REFORMULATION OF
PHYSICAL DETERMINISM

HEMPEL'S account of a regularity explanation[1] needs amplification. The usual symbolism of formal logic presents some difficulties, as it is unable to distinguish "accidental" universal statements about "closed" classes—for example, 'All my friends like coffee'—from "essential" universal statements about "open" classes—for example, 'All aqueous solutions of sodium chloride form a white precipitate with silver nitrate'. The former statements just happen to be true; my friends happen all to like coffee: but it does not follow that if Peter had been a friend, he too would have liked coffee. Whereas there does follow from a statement about an "open" class that if some thing had been a member, it would have had the property specified; if this liquid had been an aqueous solution of sodium chloride, it would have formed a white precipitate with silver nitrate.[2]

A second, logicians', difficulty is that some alleged law might be redundant because tautologous. A third, more serious, one is that for any event and any set of initial conditions there is always some relation which could be stated between them. And, indeed, for any finite number of events, and any corresponding number of sets of initial conditions, it is possible to formulate a universal law covering them all. If we are investigating the relation between two variables, we always can produce a—very artificial and complicated—function which will fit the experimental results. We have no hesitation in rejecting such functions as being entirely artificial and not representing any natural law: but we need to make this requirement explicit. Without it, physical

[1] See above, Section 8.
[2] See, for example, C. G. Hempel and Paul Oppenheim, The "Logic of Explanation", *Philosophy of Science*, 15, 1948, pp. 152–157; reprinted in Herbert Feigl and Mary Brodbeck, eds., *Readings in the Philosophy of Science*, New York, 1953, pp. 337–343.

determinism collapses into vacuity. The future always bears *some* relation to the past—namely that relation which it actually does. In order to give body to the determinist claim, we have got to say more than that. The claim would be clearest and most easily decidable if the general law were specified: but this is not done—the determinist maintains only that there are such laws, which we could *in principle* discover. In order to save the claim from vacuity we have to make some other proviso; for example, that the laws are simple. Although we have no fully formulated criteria of simplicity, and the proviso is to that extent unsatisfactory, we can apply the concept well enough in practice for it to have definite content.[1] At the very least, a function cannot be regarded as simple, unless it is calculable. The condition of simplicity secures that logical arguments based on the concept of recursiveness must apply to the functions which the determinist believes to exist.[2]

A third difficulty is an ambiguity in the application of the 'determinist' and 'determined'. We may apply these words to theories, or to the sort of events for which the theories hold good, or to a particular event for which a determinist theory holds good. Scientists often use the word 'system' for the second and third cases. No serious confusion arises from the ambiguity, but it makes for greater difficulty in understanding, especially since the word 'system' is also used by philosophers and logicians to refer to something much more a theory than an event or a sort of events, namely a formal logistic calculus—for example, the

[1] See C. G. Hempel, "Some Reflections on 'The Case for Determinism'", in Sidney Hook, ed., *Determinism and Freedom in the Age of Modern Science*, New York, 1958 and 1961, pp. 171–173 of Collier (1961) edition. See also, Bertrand Russell, "On the Notion of Cause", *Proceedings of the Aristotelian Society*, XIII, 1912–13, pp. 22–23; reprinted in *Mysticism and Logic*, London, 1953 (Penguin), pp. 192–194, and in Herbert Feigl and Mary Brodbeck, eds., *Readings in the Philosophy of Science*, New York, 1953, pp. 400–402.

[2] It might still be objected that although the general laws of nature must be expressed as calculable functions, it still could be the case that the law of development of a particular system might yet be a function which was not calculable, because of the complexity of the boundary conditions. Any *a priori* argument about the sort of functions that are calculable or not is going to run into Gödelian difficulties: but except where self-reference has been deliberately contrived, we never stray from calculable to non-calculable functions, as it were by accident.

propositional calculus described by Whitehead and Russell in *Principia Mathematica.*

A fourth difficulty comes from continuity. The account given by Hempel is a discrete one. The initial conditions either do or do not hold. The event either does or does not happen. The laws either are or are not true. But the typical theory of a natural science deals, in part, with continuous variables. The force or the acceleration in Newtonian mechanics can have any real value. And in quantum mechanics even truth and falsity are replaced by probabilities or probability-distributions. The generalisation from the discrete to the continuous case is usually not complete. So far as the question of determinism is concerned, it does not, I think, make any essential difference: but this needs to be argued for, not assumed.

These difficulties can be overcome. And it is worth surmounting them in order to face others of an altogether more formidable kind. Let us adopt the following definition for an event to be determined:[1]

If there exist premisses (1) and (2) such that

(1)   lists [a finite number of] antecedent conditions of E and is
    (i) true, and
    (ii) lists *all* the conditions relevant to E's occurrence;

and

(2)   lists law-statements relevant to E, and is such that each of its law-statements is
    (i) true,
    (ii) non-tautologous,
    (iii) universal in form,
    (iv) convertible to counterfactual form, and
    (v) simple;

and if a description of E's occurrence is deducible from (1) and (2), then E is determined.

In the continuous case, the law-statements are replaced by a set of functional dependences. Each functional dependence determines one variable in terms of a finite set of variables. That is, given the values of variables in the finite set, we can calculate the value of the one variable. Since we are dealing with phenom-

---

[1] Taken from John V. Canfield, "The Compatibility of Free Will and Determinism", *Philosophical Review*, LXXI, 1962, p. 354.

ena which are not static but change with time, one of the variables must represent time. The others describe the system at some time. If we know the values of all the relevant variables at a certain time, we have a complete description of the state of that system at that time. We could, to preserve the parallel with Hempel's account of the discrete case,[1] regard this as a [finite] set of statements assigning numerical values to certain variables $x_1, x_2, \ldots, x_n$, at a certain time and place; but usually we take it as simply a set of values for those variables. If the n variables $x_1, x_2, \ldots, x_n$ are relevant at any one time, they may be relevant at any other, and therefore we may want to know them. Thus whereas in the discrete case we only wanted to know whether or not C followed from the universal hypotheses and the initial conditions, we now want to know the value of each of $x_1, x_2, \ldots, x_n$, at any subsequent time.

A determinist system then is one in which all the relevant variables are determined by the values of some or all the variables at some previous time. If there are n relevant variables, $x_1, x_2, \ldots, x_n$, then if we know their values at time t_o, we can calculate the value of each of them at any succeeding time $t_o + t$. That is, we have that at time $t_o + t$

$$x_1 = F_1(x_{1o}, x_{2o}, \ldots, x_{no}; t)$$
$$x_2 = F_2(x_{1o}, x_{2o}, \ldots, x_{no}; t)$$
$$\cdots\cdots\cdots\cdots\cdots\cdots\cdots$$
$$x_n = F_n(x_{1o}, x_{2o}, \ldots, x_{no}; t)$$

where $x_{1o}, x_{2o}, \ldots, x_{no}$ are the values of $x_1, x_2, \ldots, x_n$ at time t_o. Thus for any given time $t_o + t$, the functions

$$x_1 = F_1(x_{1o}, x_{2o}, \ldots, x_{no}; t)$$
$$x_2 = F_2(x_{1o}, x_{2o}, \ldots, x_{no}; t)$$
$$\cdots\cdots\cdots\cdots\cdots\cdots\cdots$$
$$x_n = F_n(x_{1o}, x_{2o}, \ldots, x_{no}; t)$$

give a transformation of $x_{1o}, x_{2o}, \ldots, x_{no}$ into $x_1, x_2, \ldots, x_n$. We may ask whether this transformation is reversible: that is, given the values of $x_1, x_2, \ldots, x_n$ at time $t_o + t$, can we determine what their values must have been at t_o? It is not always possible to do this: it depends on the functions $F_1, F_2, \ldots, F_n$, whether the transformation, for a given t, is reversible. Let us write

[1] See above, Section 9.

$$x_1 = F_1^t(x_{10}, x_{20}, \ldots, x_{no}) \quad etc.,$$

to show that we are considering the transformation *for a given t*. The condition that

$$x_1 = F_1^t(x_{10}, x_{20}, \ldots, x_{no})$$
$$x_2 = F_2^t(x_{10}, x_{20}, \ldots, x_{no})$$
$$\cdots\cdots\cdots\cdots\cdots\cdots\cdots$$
$$x_n = F_n^t(x_{10}, x_{20}, \ldots, x_{no})$$

can be solved for $x_{10}, x_{20}, \ldots, x_{no}$ in terms of $x_1, x_2, \ldots, x_n$, *i.e.* that there are functions $K_1^t, K_2^t, \ldots, K_n^t$ such that

$$x_{10} = K_1^t(x_1, x_2, \ldots, x_n)$$
$$x_{20} = K_2^t(x_1, x_2, \ldots, x_n)$$
$$\cdots\cdots\cdots\cdots\cdots\cdots\cdots$$
$$x_{no} = K_n^t(x_1, x_2, \ldots, x_n)$$

is that the Jacobian

$$\begin{vmatrix} \dfrac{\partial F_1^t}{\partial x_{10}} & \dfrac{\partial F_1^t}{\partial x_{20}} & \cdots & \dfrac{\partial F_1^t}{\partial x_{no}} \\ \dfrac{\partial F_2^t}{\partial x_{10}} & \dfrac{\partial F_2^t}{\partial x_{20}} & \cdots & \dfrac{\partial F_2^t}{\partial x_{no}} \\ \cdots & \cdots & \cdots & \cdots \\ \dfrac{\partial F_n^t}{\partial x_{10}} & \dfrac{\partial F_n^t}{\partial x_{20}} & \cdots & \dfrac{\partial F_n^{\cdot t}}{\partial x_{no}} \end{vmatrix} \neq 0$$

If this condition is satisfied, we can retrodict the state of the systems at time t_0 from its state at time $t_0 + t$. But then, from the values $x_{10}, x_{20}, \ldots, x_{no}$, we have obtained we can make a further prediction to the state at time $t_0 + t'$. Hence, if the Jacobian of the transformation, at time $t_0 + t$, is non-zero, the value of the variables at any other time $t_0 + t'$ is determined. Explicitly, we have

$$x_1{}' = F_1(K_1^t(x_1, x_2, \ldots, x_n), K_2^t(x_1, x_2, \ldots, x_n), \ldots, K_n^t(x_1, x_2, \ldots, x_n), t') \quad etc.$$

It can be fairly easily shown that if we have two successive transformations of a system from its state at t_0 to its state at t, and from its state at t to its state at t', then the Jacobian of the total transformation is equal to the product of the Jacobians of the two separate transformations. So if ever the Jacobian becomes zero, then, under our restriction, it must remain zero for the transformation to all subsequent states: for the transformation from the initial state to the final state can be expressed, under the restriction, as a transformation to the "zero" state and then from that to the final state, and the Jacobian of the total transformation will be a product of two Jacobians, one of which is zero. If two or more states can, after the same interval, lead to the same result, then the Jacobian of the transformation must be zero: else we could retrodict from the result which of the two states preceded it. Similarly if a state can be followed by either of two or more states, then the Jacobian of the inverse transformations must be zero.

The set of relevant variables is only a finite set. But there are numberless ways of describing the world around us. The physical determinist believes not only that there are a finite number of physical variables required to describe a system physically, but that every other correct description follows from a complete physical description.

Although we have generalised from discrete to continuous systems in many respects, they still in some respects remain discrete. In the cases we are considering (although not in quantum mechanics) we are still dealing with only a discrete set of truth values, namely true and false, and not a continuous band of probabilities or probability-densities. More important for our later argument, the calculations are discrete. The functional dependences enable us to calculate (in principle) the value of one variable given the values of all the variables at another time, and the length of time between them: and having made this calculation, we can use the result to calculate the value of some variable at some other time again, or to calculate some dependent property of the system. But these calculations take place in a number of steps. Although functional dependences enable us to make any one of a continuous range of calculations, the calculations are themselves discrete.

§18

ARGUMENTS IN FAVOUR OF
PHYSICAL DETERMINISM

THE first argument in favour of physical determinism is that from the success of science. Scientists have been singularly successful in explaining, predicting and controlling events in the last three hundred years, and it is claimed that it is a plausible extrapolation to suppose that they will go on being successful until they have explained all there is to explain. "But" as a leading physicist has cautioned, "one must beware of supposing that one can extrapolate indefinitely the range over which reasonably accurate predictions can be made. The original evidence for predictability was experimental; other experimental evidence can, and in company with most other physicists, I believe has, disproved such an indefinite extension."[1] We may also, on a different tack, complain that scientists achieve their success in answering certain questions at the price of not addressing themselves to other questions. Many problems are ignored by the scientist on the score of their not being scientific problems. The canons of irrelevance are widely drawn. And therefore the success of science, although real, is limited.

The point is conceded, in practice, by most scientists. They admit that there are many questions they cannot answer, and that there are things they can learn from art criticism, moral philosophy, theology or politics. But the physicalist, who believes that everything can be explained in terms of physics, regards this as only a temporary imperfection.[2] When all the laws of physics are known, and all predictions can be calculated, then all questions that can be properly asked will be answerable, and all

[1] Sir George Thomson, "Determinism in Science", *Academia das Ciências de Lisboa*, IX, 1964, p. 8.

[2] See, *e.g.* J. J. C. Smart, *Philosophy and Scientific Realism*, London, 1963, ch. V; or J. J. C. Smart, "Sensations and Brain Processes", *Philosophical Review*, LXVII, 1959, pp. 141–156, esp. pp. 142–144.

that cannot be answered in his terms will be said to be un-askable, or mere coincidence. It is a Procrustean programme; but cannot be rejected simply because of that.

More telling still is the consideration that many forms of scientific explanation are not of the Hempelian form, of covering laws and initial conditions. Hardly any biological explanation is of this form, nor any geological one. Nor are most chemical ones, nor even many physical ones. Chemical explanations are very often time-independent. They show why some configuration is stable, rather than calculate how it changes with the passage of time. They are in terms of symmetries and group operators, not initial conditions and laws of development. So far as the practice of scientists go, there is little reason to fix on regularity explanation as the paradigm form of scientific explanation. Nevertheless the physicalist does so, and brushes off all other forms of scientific explanation as derivative and subsidiary. He does not disallow the questions from being asked, but is sure that he will have the answers, when his own physicalist scheme is complete.

Physical determinism is thus not a simple extrapolation from the success of science. It selects one pattern of scientific explanation in preference to others, not because the others have been found to be less successful in practice, but because the one is felt to be more explanatory in principle. There is a rational appeal about regularity explanation which makes us feel that it must be the paradigm of explanation, quite apart from any practical success it has had.[1] Moreover, materialism has great metaphysical charm. We often feel that it must be true, not because it has been borne out by science but because it seems the only possible world view. Much of the pressure towards determinism is generated by a metaphysical materialism which we find compelling on its own account, quite apart from its determinist implications.[2] In order to understand physical determinism we therefore need to appreciate the metaphysical pressures in favour of materialism.

The intellectual appeal of the world-view of Newton and Locke stems from three different sources. Locke demands a

---

[1] See above, Section 8, pp. 35–36; Section 9, pp. 38–41.

[2] The Greek Atomists and Lucretius found materialism entirely convincing, but determinism altogether unacceptable; and introduced the *clinamen* in order to be able to have the one without the other.

reductive explanation of secondary qualities in terms of primary ones.[1] And this seems right. The explanation-sketches offered by Locke,[2] and filled in by scientists in the subsequent three hundred years, seem to be just the right sort of explanation. The kinetic theory of heat, the wave theory of light, the vibration theory of sound, do have an extraordinary explanatory power. For not only do they explain common phenomena of experience, but they explain it in mathematical, and in particular, in geometrical terms, and these seem to be pre-eminently rational and illuminating. And thirdly, Newton developed his physics in terms of point-particles, and point-particles are ontologically highly satisfactory—much more so than waves or fields. Materialism—accounting for phenomena in terms of point-particles—suits our notions of what an explanation should be, because it appears to be in terms of the right sort of thing. And geometric materialism even more so.

Geometric explanations seem peculiarly explanatory because with a little training we can *see* the truth of simple geometrical truths. We can *see* that the sides of similar triangles are proportional, that the angles of isosceles triangles are equal, that corresponding angles are equal, almost that the angle subtended at the centre of a circle by a chord is double the angle subtended by the arc. Modern formalist theories of geometry, with their emphasis on proof by formal deduction from explicit axioms, play down the importance of intuition in geometry. It is of course true, as they claim, that the truth of a theorem can be established formally, and would be just as true whether we gave geometrical terms their normal geometrical interpretation or gave them any other weird interpretation which satisfied the axioms. Yet it is also true that the study of geometry began, and remains fascinating, as an articulation of certain insights into the geometrical structure of the world in which we live. Geometry is not just a formal system, one among many other formal systems, in which we happen to like deriving theorems; rather, it is a discipline in which we first have insights and arguments, and then try to formalise the arguments so as to establish their validity, and demonstrate the conclusions, beyond doubt. The Greek word for

[1] *Essay Concerning the Human Understanding*, II:8:13–25, II:23:11–12, III:6:9, IV:3:11–14, IV:3:25.

[2] *Op. cit.*, IV:3:25, IV:6:11.

proof '$\sigma\eta\mu\epsilon\hat{\iota}ov$', which means point or indication, shows this. The first geometrical proofs were ways of pointing out that the conclusion was true. To the man who doubted the truth of the conclusion one pointed out certain facts about the figure, perhaps just pointing to existing lines and angles, perhaps drawing an extra line in the sand to help him to see the figure aright, so that the truth about it should be obvious. Once he has seen it in the right *Gestalt*, he will be convinced, and forever afterwards whenever he sees a figure of the same sort, he will see it in the same way, and will *see* that the theorem about it is true. Proofs were originally not proofs in our sense but ways of communicating *Gestälten*: it was only later that Eudoxus and Euclid began, under the influence of Plato, to systematize geometry, and exhibited it as an axiomatic theory with proofs that were deductive demonstations and not merely *indications* how the figure was to be viewed so that it could be *seen* in such a light as would *show* the truth of the point in question.

Although we are now taught to put forward geometrical proofs as deductions either from axioms or from theorems already proved, the intuitive element in geometry still remains. In searching for proofs we often see it first and dress it up in proper formal style only when we come to write it down for other peoples' inspection. We do not feel we have understood a proof when we have merely followed it step by step: we want, beyond this, to be able to say 'I see it', and, in geometry at least, the word 'see' is not always being used metaphorically in this phrase. Kant's view that Euclidean geometry was a case of synthetic *a priori* truth, was not so wrong-headed as modern philosophers have tended to make out. It is true that the question whether the laws of physics will come out simpler if expressed in a Euclidean or a Riemannian space is something which cannot be settled *a priori*, and we cannot be sure that the angles of a triangle add up to *exactly* 180° and not just a tiny bit less or more, nor can we be sure that through a point there is always a line that is perfectly parallel to any given line. These are idealisations that go beyond our geometrical intuition. Our intuition provides us with an approximate geometry which we can apply approximately well to things we see, and which is approximately Euclidean. We can see that two lines are approximately at right angles to each other, that two angles are approximately equal, that a figure is approximately a circle and that one line is about twice as long as another. Moreover we can see general truths, that in so far as a figure is a parallelogram, its diagonals must intersect, or that the in-centre of an equilateral triangle must coincide with the circum-centre. These insights do not reach the standard of rigour that geometricians since Plato have hankered after, and it may be that if our experience had been very different indeed—if we had been brought up in a four-dimensional world with a hyperbolic geometry—we should have come to "*see*" things very differently. All this is conceded, and to that extent Kant's view was erroneous: but nevertheless our approximately Euclidean intuitions are insights which we do have into the world and which are neither *a posteriori* in any ordinary sense nor analytic.[1] It is in geometry, par excellence, that our mathematical notions apply immediately to the real world. We can see very easily (or, much less accurately, feel) that one line is roughly twice as long as another, whereas it is difficult to judge that one weight is twice as heavy as another, and the sentence 'this body is twice as hot as that' is nearly meaningless. Symmetry is by origin a geometrical notion. The transparent rationality that appeals to symmetry have is almost unknown to our other senses. The nearest approaches are hearing, with its recognition of pitch and harmony, and our very defective sense of what colours go with, or clash with, each other; and our discrimination of sounds and of colours seems to be not nearly so intellectual as our discrimination of shapes. Geometrical explanations, therefore, are peculiarly explanatory: they appear to be both synthetic and—to some extent—*a priori*, both empirical and rational, both concerned with the world and intellectually transparent. Even though these appearances are not fully borne out on further consideration, enough remains to make us feel that an explanation of the optical properties of a material in terms of the geometrical arrangement of the atoms of which it is ultimately composed is just what an explanation should be, and any other explanation is less satisfactory.

Locke's doctrine of substance and primary qualities showed not only a predilection for geometrical explanations, but a preference for points over (straight) lines, a preference that Newtonian mechanics fully shared. In this, too, Greek math-

---

[1] See further, J. R. Lucas, "Euclides ab Omni Naevo Vindicatus", *British Journal for the Philosophy of Science*, **20**, 1969, 1–11.

ematics led the way. Euclidean geometry is not symmetric as between points and lines. There are geometries—projective geometries—which are symmetric, or as it is technically expressed, *dual* with respect to points and lines, where if we interchanged the words 'point' and 'line' wherever they occurred in the axioms, we should get exactly the same system (in the sense that exactly the same theorems would be provable) as we had before. But Euclidean geometry is not like this. For instance, although given any two points there is one and only one line between them both, it is not true that given any two lines there is always one and only one point on them both—parallel lines never meet and so have no point that lies on them both. The original formulations of Euclidean geometry show even more clearly the preference for points over lines: lines are defined in terms of points—"a line is the shortest distance between two points"—, and are not considered to exist except when drawn between two points. Lines are defined in terms of points, and not points in terms of lines: lines have to have end-points, but points of course do not have to have end-lines. Indeed, the Greek language still more clearly favours points over lines: the word for a point, '*σημεῖον*', meant also, as we have already seen, a proof, and this root acquired a host of other meanings. Aristotle, introducing his idea of substance, says[1] '*Πᾶσα δὲ οὐσία δοκεῖ τόδε τι σημαίνειν*' which could now be paraphrased by 'Every substantive refers to a particular something' but means literally 'Every substance points to (or indicates) a something, a *this*'. There is a feeling that points are the real things which really exist, and everything else is just a pattern which lies in the eye of the beholder: and conversely, that real things must be particulars which we could point to, and that anything which we cannot point to is not really a thing, or at least not quite such a substantial thing, as things which we can point to. Plato felt the force of this line of argument, and resisted it strongly with his theory of Forms—the doctrine that particulars are not the only things to exist, but that universals also exist, and indeed are much more real and substantial things than particulars are—yet even Plato is sometimes[2] borne along by the materialist current implicit in language.

Point-particles thus are the quintessence of thinginess, the

[1] *Categories* 5, 3b10.
[2] *e.g. Sophist* 262Aff.

fundamental stuff, what the ultimate constituents of matter must turn out to be. If there is to be anything in the world—as we are sure there must be—that is hard and brute and intractable and contingent and real, then the colourless impenetrable point-particles of Locke and Newton, which can have position, mass and velocity but nothing else, are harder and bruter, and are more particular and more contingent and more un-understandable and more real, than anything else could be. If in addition the positions and velocities that each particular point-particle can have are correlated by universal laws, which seem simple and rational, and to some people so simple and rational as to be almost self-evident, then materialist explanations seem to offer the ideal explanations, which explain things without explaining them away, which make things intelligible, while still retaining an element of crude unintelligibility and brute given-ness that we associate with reality. It answers all the questions we feel entitled to ask, and then tells us, as we half expected to be told, that no more questions may be raised. We have seen as far as is permissible into the nature of things, and for the rest must be content that that is the way things are.

§19

CRITICISMS OF METAPHYSICAL MATERIALISM

ANY scheme of explanation is bound to be open to some adverse criticism, because there will be some things it cannot explain. For if it explains some things in terms of others, then these others are not themselves explained. And if it offers subsequent explanation of these in terms of yet other things, then those others in turn are left unexplained. Explanations are answers. And however many answers we give, there is always room for a further question 'Why?'. There must sometime be an end to answering. Any scheme of explanation will be unable to go on giving answers indefinitely; and when it reaches its sticking point will be open to criticism for its inability to go further.[1] It is thus not a decisive criticism of a scheme of explanation that it cannot give some sort of completely satisfactory answer. Nevertheless it is illuminating to see where each scheme breaks down.

Regularity explanations break down on the "first cause" regress. They explain events in terms of covering laws and antecedent conditions; these antecedent conditions are to be explained in terms of anterior conditions still; and these in terms of ones yet further back. Although Hempelians often speak of *initial* conditions, they never can state conditions which are, strictly speaking, initial. If time had a beginning, they might, in principle at least, follow back causes to the beginning of time, but even if they could, they would be left with an inexplicable, chance configuration of events, which they could not explain. 'At the dawn of creation', they would have to say, 'it just so happened that the point-particles came into existence in such and such positions and with such and such velocities. But don't ask me why. It is just the way it was. That is all.'

Hempelians cannot explain initial conditions. Nor should they give any account of the form of physical laws. Although the laws

[1] See also Section 11, pp. 60–61; Section 30, pp. 171–172.

of nature are more general than any state-description, they are, on the strict Hempelian account, just as contingent and rationally opaque. We cannot give any explanation of why, say, Newton's laws of motion and gravitation should be as they are, and not some other how. It is just a brute fact that the gravitational force varies inversely as the *square* of the distance, and not say, the *cube*, or the *natural logarithm*. We cannot show it to be necessary because the only sense of 'necessary', according to the Hempelians, is 'logically necessary', and if a natural law were logically necessary, it would be tautological and vacuous. The only way we can explain a natural law is by deducing it from another, as we do with Charles' gas law,[1] which we deduce from Newton's laws of motion and an assumption of perfect elasticity. But then there must be some laws, which the others are deduced from, and which are not themselves deduced from any,[2] and these, fundamental, laws would be inexplicable.[3]

It runs counter to the whole profession of materialism that much of its appeal lies in the rational appeal of the fundamental laws of nature it invokes. It must, on principle, make out the laws of nature to be rationally opaque, brute facts, without any rhyme or reason to them, which we just have to accept, and cannot seek to understand. It is a general criticism of arguments for determinism that they largely depend on rational appeal, which their avowed purpose is to show to be nugatory, and particularly so in this case, where the rational attractiveness of the fundamental laws of physics altogether belies materialism.

[1] See above, Section 17, p. 85.

[2] Strictly speaking, all we can say is that there are some, in the Latin sense of *nescioquid*, not in the Latin sense of *quidam*. In deductive systems, there must be some axioms, but we can choose which axiomatization to adopt, and what are axioms in one system may be theorems in another. In physics, however, we have not so far availed ourselves much of this possibility. We explain the gas law in terms of Newtonian mechanics, but have not attempted to explain Newton's laws by deducing them from the gas law and any other plausible assumptions.

[3] Aristotle (*Physics*, VIII, 1, 252a32ff.) makes just this criticism of Democritus, "If we make the general assumption that we have found a satisfactory principle in the fact that something is 'always' so, or will 'always' occur in such a way, we shall be mistaken. Democritus, for example, builds his theory of natural causes on the fact that things happened in the past just as they happen now. But he does not find it necessary to search for a principle which will explain this 'always'."

The rationality of Newtonian mechanics was no problem to Newton who saw it as a manifestation of the creative intellect of God. Newton's belief in God is the key to the understanding of his philosophy. He gives us a "God's eye" view of the universe, in which the whole of space at any one time is present immediately to God, who knows all the atoms individually, as it were by name, and knows where they are and what they are doing. Because God is omniscient, the God's eye view avoids all problems of epistemology. There is no problem how we come to know the underlying substance of the world, or know where it is or what it is doing. Newton views the world bathed in Absolute light, or better, illuminated by Absolute omniscience, a world of Absolute things in Absolute space, at one particular instant of Absolute time, all immediately present in God's consciousness, as it were in His *sensorium*.[1] Moreover, God, the Creator, is Himself uncreate, and not part of the created world. Newton, taking the God's eye view, always considers the world from outside. He could thus embrace materialism and mechanistic determinism as completely true, because not true of completely everything—oneself, and every thing to do with oneself, was always excepted. Like God, the thinker was not himself subject to the laws he laid down as obeyed by everything else; and awkward problems were thereby avoided.

Modern materialists profess not to believe in God, but still are "Egotheists", each one believing that he is God when he views the universe. He pictures the universe as being immediately subject to his gaze, and himself as being outside it. He can know (at least *in principle*, he will add if cautious) exactly where every thing is, and what it is doing, and this without any effort of discovery. And he puts himself outside the ambit of the laws of nature. He no longer can make an explicit exception in his own favour; but he avoids considering the awkward questions that arise if the thinker himself is part of the determined universe.

Both assumptions are wrong. Problems of epistemology cannot be evaded: exceptions in favour of oneself cannot be sustained. Even if there were no other problem of how we come to know the positions and velocities of the point-particles, we could not assume perfect precision; and that alone would be enough to rule

---

[1] *Opticks*, Query 28 and Query 31. See also, *Principia*, General Scholium.

8—F.O.T.W.

out determinism as a practical possibility.[1] Nor is the lack of exactitude merely a question of experimental error that need not concern an inerrant egotheist. The epistemology of quantum mechanics, as we shall see in the next section, and the consequences of self-reference, as we shall see in the sections after the next, establish objections to physical determinism which are objections not merely in practice, but in principle, and absolute, and fatal.

[1] Leon Brillouin, *Science and Information Theory*, 2nd ed., New York, 1962, ch. 21, Section 8, pp. 314–315; or Leon Brillouin, *Scientific Uncertainty and Information*, New York, 1964, ch. VIII, esp. Sections 3, 4, 6, 7, 8.

20

QUANTUM MECHANICS[1]

QUANTUM mechanics suggests a metaphysics less materialist than that of Locke and Newton, and is itself less mechanistic than Newtonian mechanics. But it has become less materialist in its implications by reason of a natural development of the traditional programme, and is less mechanistic just because it attempts to face the problems of epistemology that Newton burked.

Part of the attraction of Locke's programme was that secondary qualities were to be explained in terms of primary. But the success of this programme suggests another—the explanation of primary qualities in terms of something more fundamental still. We have become increasingly less willing to accept position and velocity (or, equivalently, momentum) as something basic and given and unquestionable, an unwillingness increased by our generally more critical approach to geometry. We have begun, although we have not yet carried it through, a shift of emphasis. Position and momentum are seen no longer as fundamental concepts, but as just two—an important two, but still only two— sorts of description that can be sought of a system. The fundamental concepts are no longer those of geometry and kinematics but those of functional analysis. We explain things no longer in terms of straight lines and uniform notions—primary qualities— but in terms of *eigen-values* and *orthonormal* expansions of functions—qualities a degree more intellectual still. Quantum mechanics has all the intellectual appeal of Newtonian mechanics, and rests upon an even more intellectual basis. The very same pressures which led to the acceptance of Newtonian mechanics have led also to its supersession.

Quantum mechanics not only is a theory of atoms, but incorporates a theory of light; indeed, it started as a theory of

---

[1] Quantum mechanics requires far more discussion than the brief and inevitably superficial one of this section. For a fuller treatment see Allan M. Munn, *Free-will and Determinism*, London, 1960, chs. V–VIII.

radiation. It can explain how we know where a thing is or what it is doing. But just because it can explain this, it can no longer ignore the influence our process of discovery has upon the world around us. The physicist no longer pictures to us a world of celestial objects in solemn silence all circling along their appointed paths, entirely independent of us; but tells us, rather,

> "of all the mighty world
> Of eye, and ear—both what they half create,
> And what perceive."[1]

The ontology suggested by quantum mechanics is correspondingly more difficult. Newtonian point-particles existed, had spatial position and velocity, independently of us: it made no difference to them whether we knew about them or not. But with quantum mechanical systems, our coming to know about them does make a great difference. We have lost the simple mark of existence that materialism values—complete independence of the observer. We have purchased epistemological coverage at a heavy ontological price. The epistemological price is also heavy. For the Heisenberg uncertainty principle can be regarded epistemologically, as the logical consequence of our having to interact with physical systems in order to find out things about them. It has attracted much attention. Some thinkers have claimed that it shows that even electrons have free will; more seriously, if it has been rightly interpreted, it shatters the argument from physics to determinism.

The importance of quantum mechanics for the freedom of the will is thus twofold: it requires us to form a concept of a physical system radically different from that of Newton and Locke, in which particles such as atoms and molecules obey certain laws, and it is possible to know the *state* of a physical system *completely* at one time: and it may establish a principle of physical indeterminism relevant to the behaviour of the human body. Quantum mechanics throws all the old assumptions into doubt, and makes us realise that classical materialism obtains its simple and clear-cut ontology at the cost of ignoring problems of epistemology altogether. The metaphysics suggested by Newtonian mechanics is complete and determinist only because it deals solely with material particles, and does not raise the question of how the

---

[1] *Tintern Abbey*, ll. 105–107.

initial position and velocity of a particle is to be known. Once we set out to propound a theory of matter *and* radiation which shall account not only for the things which exist independently of us but the manner in which we come to have knowledge, we can no longer indulge in an ontology which offers the ineluctable definiteness of materialism and which takes it for granted that a state of a system, independently of whether it is actually known or not, exists Out There and is in principle knowable. If we take epistemology seriously, we lose the ontological simplicity of the seventeenth century scene; and with the flooding tide of knowledge the particulate exactitude of the atoms, like the sands of the sea shore innumerable, is submerged by κυμάτων ἀνήριθμον γέλασμα.

The altered world view engendered by quantum mechanics has great consequences for our view of man. Our view of nature is likely to become more biological than mechanical. We shall no longer regard the inhabitants of the natural world as fundamentally cut-and-dried, and though we may still believe that *any* question we put to any part of nature can elicit a definite answer, we shall no longer assume that we can ask all possible questions at once.[1] I shall not, however, pursue these considerations here. We have not yet re-articulated our world-view to take account of quantum mechanics, and anything I could say would be only tentative, and unconvincing to the unconverted. Instead, I shall return to the more specific issue of the Uncertainty Principle. Some thinkers deny that it has any bearing on the freedom of the will: either because indeterminism generally is irrelevant to moral responsibility; or because quantum mechanics is, at the macroscopic level at which human being operate, effectively as determinist as Newtonian mechanics; or because quantum mechanics, although apparently indeterminist, is not, because it cannot be, really indeterminist.

The first of these objections is simply a variant on the Leucippus fallacy.[2] Just as the results of throwing a die were, on the Laplacean view, physically explicable, although mathematically random, so the behaviour of a human body may be rationally explicable, although physically random. The cunning calculating man is able to explain and predict the actions of many of his

[1] See below, Section 30, p. 167.
[2] See above, Section 11, pp. 56–59.

fellows; but finds the actions of an altruistic colleague quite inexplicable, and feels that he never knows with him what he will do. The Laplacean calculator can given good explanations of the behaviour of material objects, and make reliable predictions about them. But with human beings he never can tell what they will be up to next, nor discern any rhyme or reason in those actions they choose to perform. Yet to us, who are not limited to Laplacean or self-interested calculations, the actions of human beings generally may be intelligible, just as the actions of disinterested ones are. They may seem random from a limited viewpoint, but entirely reasonable from a more comprehensive one. Of course, the fact that they are inexplicable according to one scheme of explanation does not prove that they are explicable from some other. It only invalidates the contention that they cannot be. If human actions were completely explicable according to a physical scheme of explanation, then they could not be really explained according to a rational or human scheme of explanation. If now, however, we have shown that human actions are not completely explicable according to a physical scheme of explanation, there is no longer an argument against their being explained, as we naturally suppose them to be, according to rational or human schemes of explanation. We are using only a weak principle of double negation. We have not shown that human actions must be explicable according to rational or human schemes. But we do not need to. For we know that they are, and would never have supposed otherwise, had it not been for the arguments of the determinists.

The indeterminism of quantum mechanics does not affect ordinary macroscopic bodies, because the various minute fluctuations tend to cancel each other out, and we can have very great confidence indeed that an ordinary material object will not do anything unexpected. Unless human bodies were different from other material objects, they would be as predictable as anything else. But, of course, human bodies are different. They respond to their environment more than other bodies, far more than inanimate ones. Sometimes they respond in order to be *un*-affected by changes in the environment. Whether we are in the tropics or the arctic, the temperature of our blood remains at 98·4°F. But, just because we are in some respects immune to some changes, we are in other respects highly sensitive to those

same changes. Just because our blood-temperature does not alter
as the external temperature does, our rate of panting and
perspiration, and the dilation of our blood-vessels, varies very
much with changes of climatic conditions. Human beings are
exceptionally responsive to some sorts of "information" gleaned
from their surroundings. It makes all the difference to us whether
we hear the word 'not' or the word 'note'. A cloud no bigger than
a man's hand, or a speck on the horizon, will lead a man to alter
his actions quite radically. We are therefore highly sensitive in
some ways, although well-insulated against our environment in
others. Our nervous system seems to be much less liable to random "noise" in the ordinary transmission of messages:[1] but
there is some evidence that the threshold of sensitivity of the
retina is something well below ten quanta of light.[2] If this is so,
the theorem of large numbers does not begin to apply, and the
human body does not escape from quantum indeterminism by
reason of its macroscopic magnitude.

It is sometimes argued that quantum mechanics is not really
indeterminist itself, but only in its interpretations. If it "is considered in its wave-mechanical formulation, the state description
adopted by the theory is defined in terms of a certain function,
the so-called Psi-function. Moreover, the wave function has the
important property that given the value of this function at one
instant and assuming that the boundary conditions for the equation remain fixed, the equation assigns a unique value for that
function for any other instant. Quantum mechanics is therefore
deterministic with respect to the quantum-mechanical description of state."[3] But this argument carries little weight. "A theory
only has meaning when one is told how the symbols are to be

---

[1] John von Neumann, *The Computer and the Brain*, New Haven, 1958,
pp. 75–80.

[2] The original paper was S. Hecht, S. Schlaer and M. H. Pirenne,
"Energy quanta and Vision", *Journal of General Physiology*, 25, 1942, pp.
819–830. There have been many papers and some controversy since then.
Easily accessible accounts of the argument can be found in M. H. Pirenne,
Vision and The Eye, London, 1967, ch. VII, pp. 89–91; or in Allan M.
Munn, *Free-will and Determinism*, London, 1960, ch. VII, esp. pp. 179–
183.

[3] Ernest Nagel, *Freedom and Reason*, The Free Press, Glencoe, Ill.,
1951; reprinted in W. S. Feigl and M. Brodbeck, eds., *Readings in the
Philosophy of Science*, New York, 1953, p. 434.

interpreted. Till then it is pure thought, divorced from the external world. The interpretation is as essential a part of the theory as the mathematical analysis, and if the interpretation is in terms of probability the theory is not a deterministic one in our sense."[1]

A more radical suggestion is that quantum mechanics, although not a deterministic theory as we now know it, may be modified and expanded by the addition of some "hidden parameters" so as to become completely deterministic in the way Newtonian mechanics is. But there are two fundamental objections. If there were any hidden parameters, Pauli has shown they would have to be very well hidden indeed, not only from us but— if the expression may be excused—from the fundamental particles themselves. For these particles obey either Bose–Einstein or Fermi–Dirac statistics rather than the Boltzmann statistics we should naturally expect if each fundamental particle were an individual with a numerical identity of its own. We can make sense of this if we apply Leibniz' doctrine of the Identity of Indiscernibles, and say that there is nothing to distinguish different entities other than the physical characterization already given. If there were any hidden parameter, then, unless it were entirely otiose, there must be some occasions where the parameter takes different values although the un-hidden parameters do not. Hence there must be some cases which are not differentiated by the characterization already given, but which would be differentiated by the hidden parameter; in which case Boltzmann statistics would apply. However well hidden the hidden parameter was, it would be enough to make a logical difference between the cases and prevent us arguing against the Boltzmann statistics that the two "cases" counted as one because they were one. The only way—it seems—we can make intelligible to ourselves the applicability of the statistics which yield conclusions in fact borne out by experiment is to assume that quantum mechanics is already complete and cannot admit of any further parameters.

Moreover, not only would the addition of a hidden variable be embarrassing when we wanted to apply statistics, but, von

---

[1] Sir George Thomson, "Determinism in Science", *Academia das Ciências de Lisboa*, IX, 1964, p. 12.

Neumann has argued,[1] it would be ineffective in ironing out indeterminacies. It would not make non-commuting operators commute. Non-commuting operators will continue to have different sets of *eigen-values*, and therefore cannot both be dispersion-free, and so some probabilistic predictions will remain. Quantum mechanics, as we have it, cannot be a partial expression of a more complete system, involving further parameters, which is, when complete, deterministic. Any attempt to add such parameters to the present theory, would result in inconsistency. Unless we jettison the whole of quantum mechanics (which we can be as sure as we can be of anything that we will not ever do), we are faced with some indeterminism.

Von Neumann's proof is exceedingly difficult to follow and Pauli's argument seems tenuous to some. Many physicists are not convinced. They feel it is wrong that "God", in Einstein's words, "should play dice", and have made persistent efforts to reconstruct quantum mechanics as a deterministic theory. In this endeavour they are guided more by philosophical considerations, I think, than scientific ones, and therefore I now turn to a more general philosophical argument against determinism, which has some features in common with the quantum-mechanical critique of Newtonian mechanics, but which will apply not only to Newtonian mechanics but to any form of physical determinism, and will show that we cannot give a completely determinist account of a world that contains rational agents.

[1] John von Neumann, *Mathematical Foundations of Quantum Mechanics*, tr. Robert T. Beyer, Princeton, 1955, ch. IV, Section 2, esp. pp. 323–328. Allan M. Munn, *Free-will and Determinism*, London, 1960, ch. VI, pp. 159–161. But see also D. Bohm, "A Suggested Interpretation of the Quantum Theory in terms of 'Hidden' Variables", *Physical Review*, LXXXV, 1952, p. 166; D. Bohm, *Causality and Chance in Modern Physics*, London, 1957. For a criticism, see N. R. Hanson, "On the Symmetry Between Explanation and Prediction", *Philosophical Review*, LXVIII, 1959, pp. 353–356.

21

THE PRESUPPOSITION OF THOUGHT

MAN is not God. Although men may sometimes take a God's eye view of the universe, they cannot consistently think of themselves as not being covered by any universal account they give of the world or of humanity. For they are men, and live in the world. It is a fair criticism of many philosophies, and not only determinism, that they are hoist with their own petard. The Marxist who says that all ideologies have no independent validity and merely reflect the class interests of those who hold them can be told that in that case his Marxist views merely express the economic interests of his class, and have no more claim to be adjudged true or valid than any other views. So too the Freudian, if he makes out that everybody else's philosophy is merely the consequence of childhood experiences, is, by parity of reasoning, revealing merely his delayed response to what happened to him when he was a child. So too the determinist. If what he says is true, he says it merely as the result of his heredity and environment, and of nothing else. He does not hold his determinist views because they are true, but because he has such-and-such a genetic make-up, and has received such-and-such stimuli; that is, not because the *structure* of the universe is such-and-such but only because the configuration of only part of the universe, together with the structure of the determinist's brain, is such as to produce that result. Voltaire was contradicting himself when he wrote "I necessarily have the passion for writing this, and you have the passion for condemning me; both of us are equally fools, equally the playthings of destiny. Your nature is to do harm, mine is to love truth, and to make it public in spite of you." For if equally the playthings of destiny, then no distinction between doing harm and loving truth; nor any point in making true views public if their acceptance by men is determined by physical factors only, and not by the rational appeal of truth. In maintaining that his own views are true, Voltaire is denying that he is, along with all false believers, equally the plaything of destiny. He excepts himself. He, at least, is not determined by antecedent physical factors: he is open-minded towards the truth, and can be moved by new arguments that may occur to him. And, in publishing his views, he thinks that others too are likewise rational, and are open to rational argument, and hence not completely determined by purely physical factors.

Voltaire's successors today find their intellectual attitudes belying their determinist beliefs. They are committed to the view that whether or not determinism is true, they will believe that it is, as a result of certain physical variables having had certain values at a certain antecedent time. Even if determinism is false, they will, according to them, still say that it is true, and therefore their saying that it is true affords us no reason whatever for supposing that it really is true, but is to be construed solely as the end-product of some physical process. Yet this they are unwilling to accept. They want to be considered as rational agents arguing with other rational agents; they want their beliefs to be construed as beliefs, and subjected to rational assessment; and they want to secure the rational assent of those they argue with, not a brainwashed repetition of acquiescent patter. Consistent determinists should regard it as all one whether they induce conformity to their doctrines by auditory stimuli or a suitable injection of hallucinogens: but in practice they show a welcome reluctance to get out their syringes, which does equal credit to their humanity and discredit to their views.

Determinism, therefore, cannot be true, because if it was, we should not take the determinists' arguments as being really arguments, but as being only conditioned reflexes. Their statements should not be regarded as really claiming to be true, but only as seeking to cause us to respond in some way desired by them. And equally, if I myself come to believe in determinism, it would be because I had been subject to certain pressures or counter-pressures, not because the arguments were valid or the conclusion true. And therefore I cannot take determinism, whether in the mouth of another or believed by myself, seriously; for if it were true, it would destroy the possibility of its being rationally considered and recognised as such. Only a free agent can be a rational one. Reasoning, and hence truth, presupposes freedom just as much as deliberation and moral choice do.

This argument, which is felt by many people,[1] is also rejected by many.[2] Those who accept it, find it absolutely convincing: those who reject it, claim that it is fishy. Two objections are made. It is claimed first that the exclusive alternatives between causal explanation and rational justification assumed in the argument are not really exclusive. And it is argued secondly that all self-referential arguments, whether employed against determinists, Freudians, Marxists, or any other philosophers, are at best invalid, and probably meaningless to boot.

If the first objection is sustained and determinism is held not to preclude rational theorizing and the meaningfulness of truth, then also determinism is compatible also with moral choice and moral responsibility. Intellectual and moral reasoning are in the same case. If either presupposes freedom, then both do. And if determinism does not preclude our deciding intellectual issues on rational grounds, then neither does it our deciding practical issues on moral grounds. The only sort of determinism which can avoid being hoist with its own petard is determinism without tears. And that, as we have seen,[3] does not hold water.

[1] See J. E. McTaggart, *Philosophical Studies*, London, 1934, p. 193; "If materialism is true, all our thoughts are produced by purely material antecedents. These are quite blind, and are just as likely to produce falsehood as truth. We thus have no reason for believing any of our conclusions—including the truth of materialism, which is therefore a self-contradictory hypothesis." See also H. W. B. Joseph, *Some Problems in Ethics*, Oxford, 1931, ch. I, esp. pp. 14–15; Warner Wick, "Truth's debt to Freedom", *Mind*, LXXXII, 1964, pp. 527ff.; E. L. Mascall, *Christian Theology and Natural Science*, London, 1956, ch. 6, Section 2, pp. 212–219; J. D. Mabbott, *Introduction to Ethics*, London, 1966, pp. 115–116; C. S. Lewis, *Miracles*, London, 1947, ch. III, esp. 27; H. H. Price, *Socratic Digest*, IV, 1948, p. 98; Norman Malcolm, "Conceivability of Mechanism", *Philosophical Review*, LXXVIII, 1968, Sections 22–27, pp. 67–71.

[2] See, *e.g.*, Jonathan Bennett, *Rationality*, London, 1964, pp. 16–17; G. E. M. Anscombe, *Socratic Digest*, IV, 1948, pp. 7–15; W. H. Thorpe, "Why the Brain is more than a mere Computer", *The Times*, 25 Jan. 1969, p. 9; David Wiggins "Freedom, Knowledge and Causality", in G. Vesey, ed., *Knowledge and Necessity*, (Royal Institute Lectures), London, 1970, pp. 132–154.

[3] Section 5.

§22

SELF-REFERENCE

THE second objection, that all self-referential arguments are invalid, is one that has gained much currency in this century, on account of the paradoxes of Russell and others,[1] and Russell's solution of them. When we complain that the determinist is sawing off the branch on which he is sitting, we seem to be making much the same point as the Greeks did against Epimenides, a Cretan, who said that all Cretans were liars—meaning by 'liar' 'one who always (and not just sometimes) tells lies'—, and who by that very remark showed that he could not be telling the truth. A better version of this paradox—known sometimes as "The Liar paradox", sometimes as "Epimenides' paradox", occasionally as "The Cretan paradox"—is to consider the single utterance 'This is a lie' or, better still, 'This is false'. If it is true, then what it says is so, is so; but what it says is so is that it is false; therefore it is false. Thus if it is true, it is false. But equally, if it is false, then, what it says is so—that it is false—is so; and therefore it is true. Thus if it is false, it is true. Either way we are caught.

In his investigations into the foundations of mathematics Russell was considering the concept of a 'class'—the class of men, the class of mortals, the class of natural numbers, the class of even numbers, the class of prime numbers, *etc*. In all these examples, the class considered is quite clearly not a member of itself. I am a member of the class of men because I am a man, but

---

[1] See A. N. Whitehead and B. Russell, *Principia Mathematica*, Cambridge, Vol. I, pp. 60–65; R. Carnap, *Logical Syntax of Language*, tr. A. Smeaton, London, 1937, Section 60, pp. 211–220; F. P. Ramsey, *Foundations of Mathematics*, London, 1931, p. 27; A. Tarski, *Journal of Symbolic Logic*, 4, 1939, pp. 111–112; A. Mostowski, *Sentences undecidable in Formalized Arithmetic*, Amsterdam, 1964; see, more generally, J. F. Thomson, "On some paradoxes", *Analytical Philosophy*, 1st series, ed. R. J. Butler, Oxford, 1962, pp. 104–119 (see Corrigendum, p. viii), and J. L. Mackie, "Self-refutation—a formal analysis", *The Philosophical Quarterly*, 14, 1964, pp. 193–203.

the class of men is not itself a man and so is not itself a member of the class of men. Similarly the class of prime numbers is not a prime number and therefore not a member of the class of prime numbers. Indeed, most classes are quite clearly not members of themselves. There are some classes, however, which do appear to be members of themselves. A class, we might say, is a concept, and therefore the class of concepts, being itself a concept, was a member of the class of concepts, *i.e.* was a member of itself. Or again, more obviously, since we can clearly have classes whose members are classes—much of mathematics is about classes of classes—we can consider the class of all classes. This is a class; it is therefore a member of the class of all classes; and so it is a member of itself. With a little ingenuity it is possible to think up other examples. All such classes, however, seem somewhat unsatisfactory. Russell called them extraordinary classes, in contrast to the classes we normally consider, which he called ordinary classes. We might reasonably feel that extraordinary classes were fishy, and so decide to confine our attention to ordinary classes, and to consider only those classes which were members of the class of all ordinary classes. To make sure that all is well, we should want to know whether the class of all ordinary classes was itself an ordinary class. But if it was, then being an ordinary class it would be a member of the class of all ordinary classes, *i.e.* itself. So it would not be an ordinary class after all, but an extraordinary one. But then we argue the other way round. If it was an extraordinary class and not an ordinary one, then it would not be a member of the class of all ordinary classes, and so would not be a member of itself, which is to say that it would be ordinary. Thus we are caught either way: from the assumption that the class of all ordinary classes is itself an ordinary class, we can prove that it is extraordinary: and from the assumption that it is extraordinary, we can prove that it is ordinary. Either way we are caught. The paradox is complete.

Both paradoxes have one feature in common: somewhere or other, as the paradox is developed, some form of self-reference is involved. This naturally suggests that it is self-reference that is at fault, and if we could eliminate this, we shold avoid all paradoxes as well. Russell suggested that it was not so much *false* to talk of classes being members of themselves as *meaningless*. Although it might seem natural enough at first sight to talk of the class of all classes, and various other classes which might, or might not, be members of themselves, it was in fact meaningless to do so, just as meaningless as to talk of the number six being, or not being, green, or of a quadrilateral falling in love. Not all forms of words are either true or false. Many are nonsense, and it is only the ones which are not nonsense but meaningful that can be true or false. Moreover the bounds of meaningfulness are more closely circumscribed than is realised. It is easier to talk nonsense than one thinks. Not only must grammatical and obvious logical howlers be avoided, but one needs to be careful not to mention or presuppose any totality which in any way includes, or refers to, itself. In particular, we cannot talk of ordinary or extraordinary classes, because it is absurd to raise the question of whether a class does or does not include itself. Equally, it is meaningless to talk of the class of all classes, because this would be a totality including itself. How could one have a class of all classes? One would not have got all the classes in, until one had counted it itself in; but one would not know what *it* was, until one knew what all its members were.

Russell's objections to self-inclusive classes have considerable force when set out like this, and have been very widely accepted. There are certain difficulties: in some respects his ban on self-inclusive classes runs counter to our intuitive sense of what is plausible; and the development of mathematics becomes very complicated if we adopt his ban in all its rigour. Nevertheless, something must be done to avoid the contradictions, and it seems that self-inclusive classes are the cause of the trouble, and many versions of Set Theory (*i.e.* the Theory of Classes) obviate the trouble by following Russell and ruling out self-inclusive classes as meaningless.

The Liar paradox—"This statement is false"—is likewise generated by self-reference, the self-referential use of 'This'. The statement referred to by the phrase 'This statement' is the whole statement of which that phrase is a part. The natural objection, therefore, is that it is meaningless because the referring phrase 'This statement' fails to refer. What statement is it that is being referred to? We cannot say until we have made it, and we cannot make it unless and until we can say. Merely to utter the word '*this*' without being able to say *what*, should an enquirer ask what the reference of the word 'this' is, is simply to expend breath meaninglessly. Ryle[1] brings this out neatly, by pointing out that in all proper uses of the word 'this' we can go on and add a phrase 'namely ....' in which we explain what it is we are referring to. Thus if I was talking about Hobbes' assertion that π is equal to $3\frac{1}{8}$, I might go on to say that this statement (*i.e.* that π is equal to $3\frac{1}{8}$) is false. If I had merely said 'This statement is false' and Ryle had asked 'What statement?' I could have said what the statement was; or, to forestall such a question, I could have said at the outset 'This statement, namely that π is equal to $3\frac{1}{8}$, is false'. But if when I say 'This statement is false' I am using the word 'This' self-referentially, not, that is, to refer to some other statement, say that π is equal to $3\frac{1}{8}$, but to refer to the very statement which is being made, then I cannot forestall the question 'What statement?' by adding after the 'This' a 'namely ....' clause in which I give the statement in question; because I have not yet finished giving it, so cannot quote it until I have finished it, but cannot finish it, if I am to fill out the 'namely ....' clause, until I have quoted it. All I manage to say, if I try, is 'This statement, namely that this statement, namely that this statement ....'. Thus, whereas with all other uses of 'this' to refer to a statement, I can make sure of the reference and avoid ambiguity by quoting the statement concerned, with the self-referential use of 'this' I cannot do so; and therefore, while with all other uses of the word 'this' to refer to statements I can be sure I am not using the word meaninglessly, with self-referential uses I have no such security; and, in view of the paradoxical consequences that follow from self-referential statements, every cause for suspicion.

[1] "Heterologicality", *Analysis*, Vol. XI, 1950–51, pp. 67–68.

§23

REFERRING

RYLE's arguments, though persuasive, are not compelling. Quotation in full, although an excellent way, is not the only way of explaining the reference of the phrase 'this statement'. All we need, for the use of the word 'this' not to be meaningless, is that there should be *some* way whereby we can, if asked, explain what exactly we are referring to. It need not be by quotation in full. Indeed, except for when we are using 'this' to refer to statements or tunes, it never could. When we are speaking of things other than statements or tunes, and wish to make the reference clear, we do so by giving a description or a name, not by quoting. We can, if we wish to forestall questions, say 'this man, namely the customs official', 'this region, namely the Upper Thames Valley', or, more normally, just say 'this man', 'this region' and then if we are asked 'Which one?', answer 'The customs official' or 'The Upper Thames Valley'. This is the normal situation when we use the word 'this': it is an uncovenanted extra that in the case of statements and tunes we can in addition to describing and naming what we are referring to, also quote (or whistle) them, and if some statements should be un-quotable (or some tunes un-whistlable) it does not show that they are unreferrable to, provided that they can be referred to in some way, such as those that we use for referring to ordinary things, other than statements and tunes apart.

Thus Ryle's objection is not water-tight because there are three ways, not one, in which we can refer to a statement. These ways are:

   (i) by describing the statement
   (ii) by giving the name of the statement—*e.g.* Pythagoras' Theorem
   (iii) by quoting it.

Of these three ways, the last can be used only for statements, tunes *etc.*, and so is peculiar to them. And Ryle quite rightly notes that with self-referential statements this way is not open. But he concludes from this, wrongly, that since the referring expressions in self-referential statements cannot refer to their statements by the method which is peculiar to statements and tunes, therefore they cannot refer to them at all. This does not follow. In fact, the statement 'This statement is false' can be referred to in a variety of ways. If a person asked 'Which?', we might reply 'The statement itself, which I have just made'. Such an answer might not be acceptable, but there are yet other ways. One could describe the statement in some way, say by describing the words in some lexicographical way, or by spelling each word out. 'Which statement? The statement given by the four word sentence in which the first word is a four letter word beginning with the twentieth letter of the English alphabet and followed by ....'; or one could attach to each sentence a name or a number. We might, for instance, have a list of numbered theorems, some of which would refer to other theorems, *e.g.* Theorem 19; "Theorem 17 is provable without making use of axiom 5", and another of which would refer to itself, *e.g.* Theorem 29: "Theorem 29 is unprovable". There is the example of the Greats paper set in Oxford after the Second World War, in which question no. 13 read "Is question no. 13 a fair question?". Objection may again be made, this time on the grounds that the naming procedure has been abused. We can use names, true, in lieu of describing or quoting the thing named, but only by virtue of having once described or quoted the thing named on the occasion when it was first given its name. We do not know where the Upper Thames Valley is, or what Hobbes' assertion is, by the light of nature. Before we can use a name, the name has to be conferred, and in the process of conferring the name, the thing named has to be introduced in some other way. We can certainly in Theorem 19 speak of Theorem 17, because we have already shown what the phrase 'Theorem 17' refers to, by writing down the theorem and putting its name 'Theorem 17' against it. But do we know what 'Theorem 29' refers to? When we look to see what it names, we see what looks like a theorem, but when we look further we see that it contains a name, *viz.* 'Theorem 29' which has not yet been introduced—and one cannot call something by name until one has been introduced to it. The sceptic may justly remain suspicious of this attempt to foist self-referential statements upon him.

The sceptic's contention is clearly just, if the names are being assigned to the statements in an arbitrary manner. For any statement may have any name, and any name may refer to any statement, and there is no knowing what statement a name refers to, unless and until the statement is produced and the naming process properly carried out: and this, in the case of self-referential statements, is impossible, on the same grounds as it is impossible to fill in the 'namely . . .' clause with a quotation in full. If, however, names are assigned not in an arbitrary fashion but according to a pre-determined rule, then the sceptic's objection can no longer be maintained; for then we can know ahead of time what statement the name is going to refer to, without having to be able to produce the statement and marry it to the name before allowing it to use that name. This is the point of numbering the statements: the use of numbers suggests some determinate rule whereby the numbers are attached to the statements non-arbitrarily and so without needing a separate pairing-off process for each statement and its number. In the example sketched above, the suggestion has not been made good, as the theorems were assigned their numbers only in accordance with the order in which they were presented, which is still fairly arbitrary. But there are—and this is Gödel's great discovery—other ways of assigning numbers to statements which are essentially non-arbitrary, and whereby we have not so much assigned names to statements as have contrived for them referring expressions which refer to statements by virtue of specifying them completely. They as good as quote them, only much more economically than by means of an actual quotation, and in a way which avoids Ryle's pitfall of the statement reducing to 'This statement, namely this statement, namely this statement . . .'.

§24

GÖDEL NUMBERING AND GÖDEL'S THEOREM

GÖDEL devised a method whereby the formulae of a given formal language could be put in a 1–1 correspondence with a subset of the natural numbers: that is to say, to every number there is correlated only one formula, and to every formula there is correlated one and only one number, which we call its Gödel number. Gödel's scheme is simple. He first assigns, more or less arbitrarily, a number to each symbol of the formal language, just as we might assign numbers to the letters of the alphabet, say 1 to the letter a, 2 to b, ..., 26 to z. In this way we can replace a formula by a sequence of numbers. Gödel then, by a most ingenious device, condenses the sequence of numbers into a single number. The correlation turns on the fact that every number has a unique decomposition into prime factors (the "fundamental theorem of arithmetic"); thus

$$24 = 2^3.3^1,$$
$$2100 = 2^2.3^1.5^2.7^1,$$
$$105 = 2^0.3^1.5^1.7^1.$$

So, if we express a number in terms of its prime factors, it is uniquely determined by the exponents of the prime numbers, and if we adopt the conventions: (a) that we arrange the prime factors in order of size, (b) where a prime number is not a factor (as 2 is not a factor of 105), we insert it with a zero exponent (for $2^0 = 1$), then we have a 1–1 correlation between numbers and sequences of numbers. Going in the other direction, in order to condense a sequence of numbers—say $xyzwuvst$—into a single number, we take the first prime number –2– and raise it to the xth power, then the next –3–, and raise it to the yth power, and so on, and finally form the product, and this is the number required; thus the sequence $xyzwuvst$ would correspond to the single number $2^x.3^y.5^z.7^w.11^u.13^v.17^s.19^t$.

Thus, in two moves, first assigning numbers to the symbols, and then condensing sequences of numbers into single numbers, Gödel has succeeded in correlating numbers and formulae. The only condition required is that the formulae be only finitely long. This is a condition we should be very ready to grant; who could read an infinitely long formula, and how could we attach any meaning to it? Although the length of the formulae has to be finite, the vocabulary does not have to be finite. We can deal with an infinite vocabulary, provided that only a finite number of *arbitrary* assignments have to be made. This is the case with our formal languages. We do need an infinite number of variables of an infinite number of sorts, because we cannot antecedently set an upper bound to the number of variables a particular formula might need—if there was only a finite number, however large, there could be a formula, still only finitely long, which exhausted the available supply—but although we need infinite supplies of variables, they are all so similar that we can generate their corresponding numbers according to a standard pattern. One way is to have a symbol ′, and generate then from one base variable, *e.g.* x, x', x'', ..., *etc.* Another way, used by Alonzo Church, is to reserve the powers of 2 for the individual variables, these numbers each of them multiplied by 3 for the propositional variables, multiplied by 3×5 for the un-ary functional variables, multiplied by $3 \times 5 \times 7$ for the binary functional variables, and so on. Any regular procedure will do. Apart from the variables, there are fairly few primitive symbols, representing brackets, commas, the logicians' symbols for 'not', 'if ... then ...', and 'all', and the mathematicians' symbol for 'a is the next natural number after b'; and these few symbols can have numbers arbitrarily assigned to them.

We have succeeded in numbering the formulae of a formal language L, that is, in naming each formula not arbitrarily but in accordance with a definite convention. (The convention itself is, as we have just seen, to some extent arbitrary. But this does not matter, for we can settle the convention at the outset, and once we have done that, we shall not need to make any further arbitrary choices in assigning numbers to formulae.) In order to pursue the possibility of reproducing the Liar paradox within formal mathematics we need to follow up Gödel's scheme for correlating numbers and formulae, with a method of making up properties of numbers and relations between numbers that will correspond to logically important properties of formulae and relations between formulae. We can for instance find a property of numbers which holds of those and only those numbers that are Gödel numbers of well-formed formulae—*i.e.* not meaningless jumbles of symbols but properly constructed formulae which, we should normally say, "make sense". We can also find a function of numbers that, given the Gödel number of a formula as its argument, yields the Gödel number of the negation of that formula as its value. We should like it, especially for developing the Liar paradox, if we could find an arithmetical property of numbers that held of those and only those numbers that were Gödel numbers of true formulae of our logistic calculus. But it turns out that this is not possible. Truth—and similarly falsity— are not representable in the logistic calculus L,[1] though *provability-in-the-logistic-calculus L*—the next best thing—is.

In Gödel's theorem, therefore, the Liar paradox is altered by substituting 'un*provable-in-the-logistic-calculus-L*' for 'un*true*'. Instead of saying 'This statement is untrue' we say 'This formula is unprovable-in-the-logistic-calculus-*L*'. The effect of this emendation is twofold. First, it enables us to make the statement in entirely formalised languages: that is, it enables us to cite the formula in systems where we can use Gödel's numbering scheme to get round the ban on self-reference, and thus it enables us to produce the paradox notwithstanding any hesitations we might have in uttering statements which refer to themselves. But, in making the paradox possible, it also makes it less paradoxical. It ceases to be a contradiction. We no longer produce a statement which if true is false, and if false is true. Instead, we produce a formula which, considered as a formula of the uninterpreted logistic calculus is unprovable-in-the-logistic-calculus, but which, taken as a statement of arithmetic, must be

---

[1] See Alfred Tarski, *Logic, Semantics, Metamathematics*, tr. J. H. Woodger, Oxford, 1956, pp. 187–188 and 247; or Raymond M. Smullyan, *Theory of Formal Systems*, Princeton, 1961, ch. III, A, Section 2, Theorem 1.1, p. 45. Smullyan's approach is mathematically simpler, but conceptually more difficult. The best exposition is his "Languages in which self-reference is possible", *Journal of Symbolic Logic*, 22, 1957, pp. 55–67; reprinted in Jaako Hintikka, *The Philosophy of Mathematics*, Oxford, 1969, pp. 64–77.

true because it is the Gödel representation of a true metalogical statement.

Consider the formula which says, in effect, 'This formula is unprovable-in-the-logistic-calculus-L'. There are at first sight four possibilities. It might be true and provable-in-the-logistic-calculus-L, or true and unprovable-in-the logistic-calculus-L, or untrue and provable-in-the-logistic-calculus-L, or untrue and unprovable-in-the-logistic-calculus-L. The third possibility can can be ruled out for any reasonable logistic calculus L because we are using provable in the sense of being able to be proved to be true, so that if any formula were both untrue and provable-in-the-logistic-calculus-L, it would be both untrue and true, and the logistic calculus L would be inconsistent.[1] The first possibility can also be ruled out, because if the formula 'This formula is unprovable-in-the-logistic-calculus-L' is true, then it is un-provable-in-the-logistic-calculus-L, because that is what it says. Similarly, but conversely, the fourth possibility is eliminated, because if the formula were unprovable-in-the-logistic-calculus-L, then it would not be false but true. Thus having exhausted the other three possibilities, we are left with the case that the statement is true but unprovable-in-the-logistic-calculus-L. The argument may be put in a more direct form. If the formula were provable-in-the-logistic-calculus-L, we should have a contradiction: for, if it were provable-in-the-logistic-calculus-L, then, by the rule of double negation, it would not be unprovable-in-the-logistic-calculus-L; so that 'This formula is unprovable-in-the-logistic-calculus-L' would be false, since what it says is so, is not so: but equally, if it were provable-in-the-logistic-system, then it would be true, for to be proved is to be proved true.[2] So the

[1] See further below, Section 28.

[2] George S. Boolos, *Journal of Symbolic Logic*, 33, 1968, p. 614, criticizes my original statement of the argument here on the grounds that we can construct logistic calculi, which are syntactically consistent, but can be given an interpretation under which some theorems are false. But such possibilities are excluded by the context of the argument, where we are concerned with logistic calculi being interpreted in such a way that the propositions of simple arithmetic are true, and where the whole point of formalising the concept of provability is that nothing false shall be proved, but only truths. For a more purely syntactical approach, in which the appeal to unformalisable notions, such as truth, is reduced to a minimum, see below Section 28.

formula 'This formula is unprovable-in-the-logistic-calculus-L' is not provable-in-the-logistic-calculus-L, but unprovable-in-the-logistic-calculus-L. Further, if the formula 'This formula is unprovable-in-the-logistic-calculus-L' is unprovable-in-the-logistic-calculus-L, then it is true that that formula *is* unprovable-in-the-logistic-calculus-L; that is, 'This formula is unprovable-in-the-logistic-calculus-L' is true. This, although paradoxical, is not a contradiction. Instead of having emeshed ourselves in contradictions, we shall have shown something very surprising about mathematical systems in general, namely that they are incomplete. Every serious mathematical system has some statements in it, which cannot be proved in it, but which we should have to agree were true.

This is far from what we should have expected, but it follows, provided that we can find an arithmetical property of numbers which holds of those and only those numbers that are Gödel numbers of formulae provable-in-the- (given-)system.

The details of Gödel's argument are tedious, and the rigorous proof is extremely laborious:[1] but its validity is beyond doubt. It establishes for all logistic calculi (or formal systems[2]) which are both consistent and adequate for simple arithmetic—*i.e.* contain the natural numbers and the operations of addition and

[1] Kurt Gödel, "Über formal unentscheidbare Sätze der Principia Mathematica und verwandter Systeme," Part I, *Monatshefte für Mathematik und Physik*, Vol. XXXVIII (1931), 173–198. English translation, Kurt Gödel, *Lectures at Institute of Advanced Study*, Princeton, N.J., 1934; or by B. Meltzer, Edinburgh, 1962 (but see review in *Journal of Symbolic Logic*, 30, 1965, pp. 357–359). See also Ernest Nagel and J. R. Newman, *Gödel's Proof*, New York, 1958, London, 1959; J. Findlay, "Goedelian Sentences: a Non-Numerical Approach", *Mind*, LI, 1942, pp. 259–265; Norwood Russell Hanson, The Gödel theorem: "An informal exposition", *Notre Dame Journal of Formal Logic*, 2, 1961, pp. 94–110, and p. 228 (but see review by Alonzo Church, *Journal of Symbolic Logic*, 27, 1962, pp. 471–472); László Kalmár, "A simple Construction of Undecidable Propositions in Formal Systems", *Methodos*, 2, 1950, pp. 227–231. P. J. FitzPatrick, "To Gödel via Babel", *Mind*, LXXV, 1966, pp. 332–350; H. Lacey and G. Joseph, "What the Gödel Formula Says", *Mind*, LXXVII, 1968, pp. 77–83.

[2] The phrase 'formal system' is in more general use and is more readily understood. But the word 'system' is also used in a different sense in 'physical system', and in order to avoid confusion I use 'logistic calculus' instead of 'formal system' except where the context is quite clear. See above, Section 18, pp. 91–92.

multiplication—a partial analogue of the Liar paradox. Every such logistic calculus contains formulae which, though perfectly meaningful, are unprovable-in-the-logistic calculus; and some of which, moreover, we, standing outside the logistic calculus can see to be true.

§25

THE APPLICATION OF
GÖDEL'S THEOREM[1]

GÖDEL'S theorem applies to physical determinist systems,[2] which are sufficiently rich to contain an analogue of simple arithmetic.[3] Human beings can do simple arithmetic: they can count, they can add, they can multiply. Any physicalist description of a human being, if it is not to be patently inadequate, must contain descriptions of behaviour which we should regard as uttering or writing numerals, and must contain, as a sub-class of causal processes that can occur, processes which we should regard as calculating a sum or a product. Of course, given any particular description of a human being and his environment, it does not follow that he will utter every number, or perform every

[1] For a shorter version of this argument, see J. R. Lucas, "Minds, Machines and Gödel", *Philosophy*, XXXVI, 1961, pp. 112–127; reprinted in Kenneth M. Sayre and Frederick J. Crosson, eds., *The Modeling of Mind*, Notre Dame, 1963, pp. 255–271; and in Alan Ross Anderson, ed., *Minds and Machines*, Englewood Cliffs, 1964, pp. 43–59: see also, Ernest Nagel and James R. Newman, *Gödel's Proof*, London, 1959, ch. VIII, pp. 100–102. Paul Rosenbloom, *Elements of Mathematical Logic*, pp. 207–208. Hartley Rogers, *Theory of Recursive Functions and Effective Computability*, New York, 1958, and K. R. Popper, "Indeterminism in Quantum Physics and Classical Physics", *British Journal for the Philosophy of Science*, Vol. I, 1951, pp. 179–188.

[2] See above, Section 17, pp. 91–92.

[3] Dr. J. Bronowski, of the Salk Institute, has pointed out that Gödel's theorem requires us to have the natural numbers, and not merely the real numbers. We take it for granted that the former are logically prior to the latter; but so far as the physical world is concerned it may be, *pace* Kroeneker, the other way about. Plato, in his doctrines of τὸ πέρας and τὸ ἄπειρον, and of the One and the infinite Dyad, may have had some intimations of this. So long as we have the operations of subtraction and division defined over the real numbers—so long as the real numbers form a field—we can define natural numbers in terms of them. And for our present argument it would be enough to observe that the natural numbers are embedded in the foundations of all *human* thinking.

addition or every multiplication; indeed, he could not do any of these in the confines of his limited life-time. But given any particular description of a particular human being, then for *some* descriptions of possible environments, he must be able to utter or write numerals, and perform additions and multiplications. For a human being who could not, when asked in suitable circumstances, say what the next number after a given number was, or what a certain sum or product was, would be, at least, a mathematical blockhead. And not all men are dunces.

The physical determinist, therefore, must represent at least some persons by a physical description which will, in conjunction with some description of a possible environment, have as a consequence, in accordance with the laws of nature, a description of their uttering or writing a numeral, or of their calculating a sum or a product. The alleged physical description of any particular human being will, more generally, fix what descriptions of subsequent states or processes can occur in some circumstances, and which of these are to be regarded as uttering statements or writing formulae (of any sort), or making calculations or drawing inferences (of any sort). Moreover, on the view of the physical determinist, there are only a finite number of circumstances—possible environments—that are discriminably different. For there are only a finite number of independent variables, and although, considerations of quantum mechanics apart, these are thought to vary continuously, very small differences, at least in the environment, are not perceived by the human organism, and make no difference to its responses. We have therefore only a definite finite number, although a very large one, of possible circumstances affecting a particular human being. And therefore we have only a definite finite set, although a very large one, of the *kinds* of process which, according to the physical determinist, a human being can do, and which we should recognise as mathematical calculations or inferences. Note that we say kinds of process, kinds of inference. Under the condition of mortality, there is a limit to the number of actual processes that a particular human being will undergo, and to the number of inference-*instances* that he will perform. But we have considered a particular human being not in particular circumstances, but in all possible ones; we consider, that is, any instance satisfying that description-*type* which, the physical determinist alleges, completely describes a particular human being, in all possible circumstance-*types*. And we say there are only a definite finite number of kinds of process that, according to the physical determinist, can go on, and so, only a definite finite number of types of inference that any particular human being can draw.[1]

Similar reasoning establishes that there is only a definite finite number of beliefs which, according to the physical determinist, a particular human being can be said to hold. If this is so, the reasoning of any particular human being can be viewed as a logistic calculus (different for different human beings): the beliefs held at the outset are the "initial formulae" ("primitive propositions", "postulates" or "axioms"); and the types of inference drawn by that particular person (whether or not we regard them as valid, sound, or cogent) will be the "rules of inference". Thus each human being's reasoning, if he can really, as the physical determinists allege, be completely described in physical terms, may be viewed as a proof-sequence in some logistic calculus.[2] We have formulae representing the state of the particular human being before and after each inference, and we note what kind of process it is that leads from the one to the other. We can thus represent every single inference and every sequence of inferences that the human being might perform. This representation would be a formal proof of the description of the end state from that of the initial state, by virtue of the rules of inference. For we shall have a proof-sequence of formulae, each succeeding one of them being written down in virtue of some rule of inference having been applied to some previous formula or formulae (except, of course, for the initial formulae, which are

---

[1] For the distinction between type (or kind, or sort) and instance (or token) see C. S. Pierce, *Collected Works*, Cambridge, Vol. 4, p. 537; Susan Stebbing, "Sounds, Shapes and Words", *Proceedings of the Aristotelian Society*, Supplementary Volume XIV, 1935, p. 4; A. M. MacIver, "Token, Type, and Meaning", *Analysis*, 4, 1937, pp. 58–64; Max Black, "Some Problems connected with Language", *Proceedings of the Aristotelian Society*, XXXIX, 1938–9, pp. 46–49; or J. R. Lucas, "Causation", in *Analytical Philosophy*, 1st series, ed. R. J. Butler, Oxford, 1962, pp. 35–37.

[2] The late Mr. E. J. Lemmon, of Trinity College, Oxford, questioned my viewing reasoning as a proof-sequence rather than a computation. But the two are equivalent. See, for example, A. A. Markov, in *Véstnik Akadémii Nauk SSSR*, Vol. 27, no. 8, 1957, pp. 21–25.

given because they represent the initial beliefs of the human being in question). The conclusions which, according to the physical determinist, a particular man can produce as true will therefore correspond to the theorems that can be proved in the corresponding logistic calculus. We now construct a[1] Gödelian formula in this logistic calculus, say L, which cannot itself be *proved-in-the-logistic-calculus-L*. Therefore the particular human being who is, according to the physical determinist, represented by the logistic calculus L, cannot produce such a formula as being true. But he *can* see that it is true: any rational being could follow Gödel's argument, and convince himself that the Gödelian formula, although unprovable-in-the-logistic-calculus-L, was nonetheless —in fact, for that very reason—true. Therefore a human being cannot be represented by a logistic calculus, and therefore cannot be described completely in terms of physical variables, all of whose values are completely determined by the conjunction of their values at some earlier time.

[1] The construction of the Gödelian formula depends on the assignment of Gödel numbers which is (pp. 124–125) more or less arbitrary. Hence there are for any given logistic calculus infinitely many Gödelian formulae, and we should talk of 'a' rather than 'the'. But the argument will not be affected if we assume—as most writers do—that the Gödel numbering convention has been fixed once and for all.

OBJECTIONS TO THE
GÖDELIAN ARGUMENT

THE application of Gödel's theorem to refute physical determinism has been much criticized. The objections fall into three groups. It is objected, first, that too formal and deductive a characterization of human reasoning has been given: Gödel's theorem may apply to a calculus of deductive inferences, but most human thinking is informal and not confined to deductive patterns. Secondly the argument itself is often misconstrued. It is what I shall term a "dialectical" argument, and it depends on a certain interplay between formal and intuitive elements, and many critics have missed the point. It is possible to reconstruct the argument more formally, but then there are a third group of objections to the use made of the notions of consistency and truth.

Human beings are not confined to making deductive inferences, and many philosophers have claimed that we could give a complete description of a human being in physical terms in which his reasoning was not represented by a formal, logistic calculus, or, what comes to the same thing, construct a computer which could make non-deductive inferences, and thus, perhaps, escape the Gödel result.[1] Or, alternatively, reasoning should be represented, not by one formal deductive logistic calculus, but by a whole series of them, and thus be able to transcend the limitations on any one.[2]

Any such proposal runs into the difficulty that if it is sufficiently determinate to support physical determinism, and sufficiently

[1] C. G. Hempel, in private conversation; Hartley Rogers, *Theory of Recursive Functions and Effective Computability*, Massachusetts Institute of Technology (mimeographed), 1957, pp. 152ff. F. H. George, "Minds, Machines and Gödel", *Philosophy*, 1962, pp. 62–63. C. H. Whitely, "Minds, Machines and Gödel", *Philosophy*, 1962, pp. 61–62. J. J. C. Smart, *Philosophy and Scientific Realism*, London, 1963, pp. 119–120; see also J. J. C. Smart, *Synthese*, Vol. XIII, no. 2, June 1961, pp. 108–110.

[2] Hao Wang, in private conversation.

careful to avoid inconsistency, it provides enough logistic structure for Gödel's argument to apply. Many cyberneticians have suggested the use of randomising elements in computers; and, in view of quantum mechanics, it is entirely reasonable to incorporate them into a physical description of a human being. But if a computer, or an instance of a physical description, just works at random, although it is non-deductive all right, it is no model for a human being with a mind; nor again if it is, or is like, an ordinary computer together with a few randomising devices, selecting from a range of alternatives sufficiently circumscribed to avoid inconsistency; for Gödel's theorem would still apply to the logistic calculus formed by the disjunction of all the permissible alternatives. Nor again, if the machine were programmed, as Hartley Rogers suggests, to entertain various propositions which had not been proved or disproved, and on occasion add them to its list of axioms: for it cannot accept all unprovable formulae, and add them to its axioms, or it will find itself accepting both the Gödelian formula and its negation, and so be inconsistent. Nor would it do if it accepted the first of each pair of undecidable formulae, and, having added that to its axioms, would not longer regard its negation as undecidable, and so would never accept it too: for it might happen on the wrong member of the pair: it might accept the negation of the Gödelian formula rather than the Gödelian formula itself. And the logistic calculus constituted by a normal set of axioms with the negation of the Gödelian formula adjoined, although not inconsistent, is an unsound logistic calculus, not admitting of the natural interpretation. It is something like non-Desarguian geometries in two dimensions: not actually inconsistent, but rather wrong, sufficiently much so to disqualify it from serious consideration. Careful criteria of selection of unprovable formulae will be needed. Hartley Rogers suggests some possible ones. But once we have rules generating new axioms, even if the axioms generated are only provisionally accepted, and are liable to be dropped again if they are found to lead to inconsistency, then we can set about doing a Gödel on this system, as on any other. In short, however a computer is designed or a physical system described, it must proceed either at random or according to definite rules. In so far as its procedure is random, we cannot outsmart it; but its performance is not going to be a convincing parody of intelligent behaviour: in so far as its procedure is in accordance with definite rules, the Gödel method can be used to produce a formula which the computer according to those rules, or the physical system according to its description, cannot assert as true, although we, standing outside the system, can see it to be true.[1]

Further, vaguer, claims are sometimes made on behalf of computers. It is suggested that cyberneticians might be able to construct self-programming, self-organizing entities, which are not wholly specified in advance, not even determined by their original programme together with their environment.[2] So far, we have constructed only fairly simple and predictable artefacts. When we increase the complexity of our computers there may, perhaps, be surprises in store for us. Turing draws a parallel with a fission pile.[3] Below a certain "critical" size, nothing much happens: but above the critical size, the sparks begin to fly. So too, perhaps, with human beings and computers. Most human beings and all computers are, at present, "sub-critical"—they react to incoming stimuli in a stodgy and uninteresting way, have no ideas of their own, can produce only stock responses—but a few human beings at present, and possibly some computers in the future, are "super-critical", and scintillate on their own account. Turing is suggesting that it is only a matter of complexity, and that above a certain level of complexity a qualitative difference appears, so that "super-critical" computers will be quite unlike the simple ones hitherto envisaged. So too, a physi-

---

[1] Gödel's original proof applies if the rule is such as to generate a primitive recursive class of additional formulae; see Proposition VIII and fn. 53 on p. 193 of his original paper, "Über formal unentscheidbare Sätze der Principia Mathematica und verwandter Systeme", Part I, *Monatshefte für Mathematik und Physik*, Vol. XXXVIII, 1931; English translation, by B. Meltzer, Edinburgh, 1962, p. 65; or see Section 1 *init.* and Section 6 *init.* of Gödel's *Lectures at the Institute of Advanced Study*, Princeton, N.J., 1934. It is in fact sufficient that the class be recursively enumerable. See J. Barkley Rosser, "Extensions of some theorems of Gödel and Church", *Journal of Symbolic Logic*, I, 1936, pp. 87–91.

[2] F. H. George, "Minds, Machines and Gödel", *Philosophy*, XXXVII, 1962, pp. 62–63.

[3] "Computing Machinery and Intelligence", *Mind*, LIX, 1950, p. 454; reprinted in James R. Newman, *The World of Mathematics*, IV, New York, 1956, pp. 2117–2118; and in Alan Ross Anderson, *Minds and Machines*, Englewood Cliffs, N.J., 1964, p. 25.

calist might contend that human beings were capable of being described completely in purely physical terms, but that the system was so complicated, that it was impossible even in principle to predict precisely what it was going to do. Putnam has considered "machines" that are not Turing machines, but exemplify the calculus of EA predicates.[1] EA predicates express in mathematical logic James Russell Lowell's conviction that although Truth was continually on the scaffold, Wrong for ever on the throne, yet ultimately, in the long long run, Truth would triumph, and stay triumphant. We can never tell with an EA machine whether it is going to get the answer right this time or not, but only predict that ultimately it will be guided into all truth, in spite of indefinitely many manifestations of fallibility *en route*. There is no *a priori* reason why exemplifications of EA predicates should not be produced. But they are not determinist systems, and to use them as models for human beings is to abandon physical determinism. It is essential to determinism that humans being operate according to "physical principles", that is, that the operation of the whole is determined, in virtue of the laws of nature, by the initial condition of the physical constituents described in physical terms. It is how a system behaves that counts, not what it is made of. Perhaps one day there might be produced a computer which was so complicated that it ceased to be predictable, even in principle, and started doing things on its own account, or, to use a very revealing phrase, it might begin to have a mind of its own. It would begin to have a mind of its own when it was no longer entirely predictable and entirely docile, but was capable of doing things which we recognised as intelligent and not just mistakes or random shots, but which we had not programmed into it. But then it would cease to be a computer within the meaning of the act, no matter how it was constructed. We should say, rather, that we had created a mind, in the same sort of sense as we procreate people at present. There would then be two ways of bringing new minds into the world, the traditional way, by begetting children born of women, and a new way of constructing very, very complicated systems of, say, valves and relays. When talking of the second way, we should take care to stress that although what was

[1] See E. M. Gold, "Limiting Recursions", *Journal of Symbolic Logic*, **30**, 1965, pp. 28–48; and H. Putnam, "Trial and Error Predicates", *Journal of Symbolic Logic*, **30**, 1965, pp. 48–57.

created looked like an artefact, it was not one really, because it was not just the total of its parts. One could not tell what it was going to do merely by knowing the way in which it was built up and the initial state of its parts: one could not even tell the limits of what it could do, for even when presented with a Gödel-type question, it got the answer right. In fact we should say briefly that any system which was not floored by the Gödel question was *eo ipso* not a Turing machine, *i.e.* not a computer within the meaning of the act.

§27

DIALOGUES AND INTUITIONS

THE Gödelian argument is easily misunderstood: partly because it is dialectical[1] in structure, partly because it depends at two points on men being reasonable in an intuitive but unformalisable way. The argument is not a direct proof of the universal negative proposition "No human being can be completely described in purely physical terms", but a schema of refutation which, I hold, an intelligent man can adapt to refute any particular claim that a particular human being is completely described by a given, purely physical, description. Because the argument is *dia*lectical —between two parties, perhaps different people, perhaps just me and my *alter ego*—it will work where no straightforward monologue of proof-sequences will apply, and it will draw finer distinctions than any monologous argument can: but equally, it will depend on the two parties "playing the game" and will lack the coercive force of traditional, monologous, deductive logic.

A dialogue is something like a game. In this case the physical determinist makes the first move, claiming that human beings can be completely described in purely physical terms I (taking on myself the role of the anti-determinist) have the second move and instance a particular man—possibly myself, possibly some one else. What sort of physical system, represented by what logistic calculus, does the determinist claim that this particular man is? It is then the determinist's turn again, and it is up to him to give the specification which, in his opinion, characterizes the particular man in question. Only then will there be purchase for the Gödelian argument, which has to be adapted in an unspecifiable

---

[1] I have tried to elucidate the distinctive features of dialectical arguments elsewhere: see "The Lesbian Rule", *Philosophy*, XXX, 1955, pp. 202–206; "On Not Worshipping Facts", *Philosophical Quarterly*, **8**, pp. 144–146; "The Philosophy of the Reasonable Man", *Philosophical Quarterly*, **13**, 1963, pp. 103–105 and especially "Not 'Therefore' but 'But'", *Philosophical Quarterly*, **16**, 1966, pp. 281–307.

way to take account of the exact form of the specification offered by the determinist in his second move.

The argument is more economical than a direct disproof could be. It does not require "that all men, being in principle rational, can follow Gödel's argument and produce as true the Gödelian formula of every machine",[1] but only that there should be some man who can follow Gödel's argument, and, if told that any particular logistic calculus L represents his intellectual output, produce as true the Gödelian formula of L. Provided only one man could be sure of finding a Gödelian heel in each particular determinist Achilles he was alleged to be, it would be enough to show physical determinism false. For determinism can admit of no exceptions. If it cannot make good its claim to account for the intellectual output of every single human being, its spell is broken. It does not matter that there are many human beings who cannot follow Gödel's arguments, for those who cannot resemble those who can in very many important ways, and once we have shown that some people cannot be completely explained in physical terms, we shall have no hesitation in concluding that none can.

Because the argument is in dialectical form, it can draw very fine distinctions between the different senses of *all, every, each, any, a,* and *one,* and can deal with the difficulties of those physicalists who believe that they can describe and explain in physical terms *any* piece of human behaviour, and so must be able to describe and explain it *all.* But that does not follow. For any natural number there is a greater, but it does not follow, and is not true, that there is a natural number greater than them all. So too, a physicalist, finding a formula which cannot be produced as true by the physical system he has described, may concede that his description was inadequate, but seek to amend it, and make it a more adequate one, in which the formula can be produced as true. He can indeed do this; but then the second system will have a Gödelian formula all of its own, constructed by applying Gödel's procedure to the formal logistic calculus which represents the reasoning of a particular human being according to the revised description offered by the physicalist. And this second formula will be one which even an instance of the revised physical

---

[1] K. M. Sayre and F. J. Crosson, eds., *Philosophy and Cybernetics,* Notre Dame, 1967, p. 22.

description will be unable to produce as true, although a rational human being will be able to see that it is true. And so it will go on. However complicated we make our description of a particular man, the part of it that claims to describe his reasoning processes will correspond to a formal logistic calculus, which will be liable to the Gödelian procedure for finding a formula unprovable-in-that-logistic-calculus. Nothing that is adequately and completely described by the physical description will be able to produce this formula as being true, although the human being, supposed to be adequately described by the physical description will be able to see that it is true. Therefore the description is not adequate. And any description offered by the physical determinist—however much he adds to it—will thus be found to be incomplete. He is trying to produce for a human being a description which is purely physical—which is essentially "dead"; but being in fact alive, the person described can always go one better than a formal, ossified, dead description can allow for. Thanks to Gödel's theorem, the human being always has the last word.

This is the answer to one objection put forward by Turing, Benacerraf and Good. Turing argues that the limitation set by Gödel's theorem to the intellectual powers of a physical system or a machine does not amount to anything much. Although each individual physical system or machine is incapable of getting the answer to some questions, each individual human being is, after all, fallible also: and in any case "our superiority can only be felt on such an occasion in relation to the one machine over which we have scored our petty triumph. There would be no question of triumphing simultaneously over *all* machines"[1] But this is not the point. We are not discussing whether machines or men are superior, but whether they are the same. In some respects machines are undoubtedly superior to human beings; and the question on which they are stumped is, admittedly, a rather niggling, even

[1] A. M. Turing, "Computing Machinery and Intelligence", *Mind*, LIX, 1950, p. 445; reprinted in James R. Newman, *The World of Mathematics*, IV, New York, 1956, p. 2110; and in Alan Ross Anderson, *Minds and Machines*, Englewood Cliffs, N.J., 1964, p. 16. Paul Benacerraf, "God, the Devil and Gödel", *The Monist*, 51, 1967, pp. 22–23. I. J. Good, "Human and Machine Logic", *British Journal for the Philosophy of Science*, 18, 1967, pp. 145–146. David Lewis, "Lucas against Mechanism", *Philosophy*, XLIV, 1969, pp. 231–233. David Coder, "Gödel's Theorem and Mechanism," *Philosophy*, XLIV, 1969, pp. 234–235.

trivial, question. But it is enough, enough to show that the machine is *not the same* as a man. True, the machine can do many things that a human being cannot do: but if there is of necessity something that the machine cannot do, though the man can, then, however trivial the matter is, we cannot equate the two, and cannot hope ever to have a physical system that will adequately represent the man in question. Nor does it signify that it is only an individual physical system or machine we have triumphed over: for the triumph is not over only *an* individual physical system or machine, but over *any* individual that anybody cares to specify—in Latin *quodvis* or *quodlibet*, not *quoddam*—and a physical specification of a man must be an individual physical system or machine. Although it is true that any particular "triumph" of a man over a physical system or machine could be "trumped" by another physical system or machine able to produce the answer the first physical system or machine could not produce, so that "there is no question of triumphing simultaneously over all machines", yet this is irrelevant. What is at issue is not the unequal contest between one man and all physical systems, but whether there could be any, single, physical system that could do all a man can do. For physical determinism to hold water, it must be possible, in principle, to specify *a* physical system—*any*, but only a *definite one*—which can do everything the man in question can do. I point to something the physical system cannot do but the man can. The determinist cannot say "that a machine could do that as well"[1] for it is *another* machine, and what we were arguing about was whether the machine or physical system *as originally specified* was equivalent to a man. Of course, the determinist may be allowed to revise his claim and modify his specification, but each time he does so, I am entitled to look for defects in the new specification. If the determinist can devise a specification that I cannot find fault with, his thesis is established: if he cannot, then it is not proven; and since—as it turns out—he necessarily cannot, it is refuted. To succeed, he must be able to produce some definite physical specification of the man—any one he likes, but one he can specify, and will stick to. But since he cannot, in principle cannot, produce any physical specification that is adequate, even though the point of failure is a

[1] Paul Benacerraf, "God, the Devil and Gödel", *The Monist*, **51**, 1967, p. 22, line 36.

minor one, he is bound to fail, and physical determinism must be false.

It may yet be objected that the procedure whereby the Gödelian formula is constructed is a standard procedure—only so could we be sure that a Gödelian formula can be constructed for every formal logistic calculus. But if it is a standard procedure, then it should be able to be embodied in a physical process and incorporated into that physical system which is allegedly a human being. We could describe a physical system which not only could perform the normal inferences, represented by a formal logistic calculus, but also go through Gödel's procedure, and then produce the conclusion of that procedure as being true; and then repeat the procedure as often as required. This would correspond to having a formal logistic calculus with an additional rule of inference which allowed one to add, as a theorem, the Gödelian formula of the rest of the formal logistic calculus, and then the Gödelian formula of this new strengthened formal logistic calculus, and so on. It would be tantamount to adding to the original formal logistic calculus an infinite sequence of axioms, each the Gödelian formula of the formal logistic calculus hitherto obtained. Yet even so, the matter is not settled: for the physical system described as being capable of the Gödelising process, as we might call it, is a *different* physical system from those described without such a capacity; and although a physical system capable of the Gödelising process would be able to do just those things wherein the inadequacy was revealed of those without it, yet we might expect a person, faced with a description which included a Gödelising process to take this into account, and out-Gödel the new description, Gödelising process and all. This, in fact, is so. Even if we adjoin to a formal logistic calculus the infinite set of axioms consisting of the successive Gödelian formulae, the resulting formal logistic calculus is still incomplete, and contains a formula which cannot be proved-in-the-logistic-calculus, although a rational being can, standing outside the logistic calculus, see that it is true.[1] We had expected this, for even if an

[1] Again, Gödel's original proof clearly applies since the successive Gödelian formulae are a primitive recursive class. See Proposition VIII and fn. 53 on p. 193 of Gödel's original paper, "Über formal unentscheidbare Sätze der Principia Mathematica und verwandter Systeme", Part I, *Monatshefte für Mathematik und Physik*, Vol. XXXVIII, 1931;

infinite set of axioms were added, they would have to be specified by some finite rule or specification, and this further rule or specification could then be taken into account by a mind considering the enlarged logistic calculus. In a sense, just because a human being has the last word, he can always pick a hole in any description presented to him as a description of himself. The description must be, in some sense, finite and definite: and then the person described can always go one better.

Is it fair always to claim the last word? Many of the prediction-paradox arguments against determinism depended on having the last word, and often their claim seemed dubious. The Gödelian argument, however, is not a prediction paradox. It is a timeless argument about the logical possibilities of a logistic calculus, any logistic calculus satisfying a certain sort of description, not a tensed prediction which could well be rendered inapplicable by a further piece of information. Arguments based on self-prediction have, for this reason, the same unconvincing trickiness about them as do the paradoxes of self-reference. But just as Gödel's theorem, although fundamentally based on a sort of self-reference, escapes being fallacious, so does this application of it. It might well be that in learning Gödel's theorem our brains undergo a significant change of state; possibly even of structure: and it is right to regard details about the specification of the systems as further information. Nonetheless, Gödel can still out-Gödel a specified physical system supposed to have the same structure and provided with the same information as himself: for the further information given in providing details about the specification of the physical system is given once for all—this follows from the fact that the physical system has a determinate structure which we have specified. We therefore avoid the endless attempts to jump on one's own shadow that the prediction paradox involves. Moreover, even if the physical system had become capable of "doing Gödel's theorem", *i.e.* of classifying as true the Gödelian sentence relative to its former system of elementary mathematics, Gödel can out-Gödel that. For Gödel can *go on*: whereas the system described in purely physical terms, because it has a definite specified structure, cannot go on indefinitely.

English translation, by B. Meltzer, Edinburgh, 1962, p. 65; or see Section 1 *init.* and Section 6 *init.* of Gödel's *Lectures at the Institute of Advanced Study*, Princeton, N.J., 1934.

The reason why Gödel, and other human beings, can go on, while systems described in purely physical terms cannot, is that there are two senses of the term 'Gödelian argument'. It may mean an argument according to an exact specification—*e.g.* taken from Gödel's original paper: or it may mean a Gödel-type argument, similar to Gödel's original argument in certain important respects, but not completely, or altogether exactly, specified. The former—the exactly specified argument—can be programmed into a machine or incorporated into a description in purely physical terms: the latter—the not altogether exactly specified one—cannot. I claim that a human being can understand or get the hang of the latter, its incompletely exact specification notwithstanding, whereas all we can ever reproduce in a machine, or in a description in purely physical terms, is the former. It is like Mathematical Induction. A machine can carry out any finite number of inferences, and therefore can prove a formula for any particular finite number, but cannot "see", as a human mathematician can, that we can therefore generalise and say that the formula holds for every natural number. In a somewhat similar way, human beings are able not only to follow particular Gödelian arguments, but to generalise and "see" that Gödel-type arguments in general are applicable and are valid.[1] It is their grasp of the Gödelian argument in this latter sense which enables human beings to outwit machines and show all purported descriptions of themselves to be incomplete. Human beings, because they are rational, do not have to proceed according to the rule-book, whereas the whole programme of physical determinism is to reduce everything to regularities and rule-bound phenomena. The physical determinist, by his very profession of faith, has no room for the intuitive grasp of the understanding. But we, being rational, albeit only imperfectly so, can get the hang of ideas without any rule being given us, just as we can recognise the truth of a proposition although it cannot be proved within the given logistic calculus. This is what it is to be rational. This is why being rational we are entitled to the last word, and can always show ourselves cleverer than our denigrators thought.

[1] See further, J. R. Lucas, "Mechanism: a Rejoinder", *Philosophy*, XLV, 1970, pp. 149–151.

28

MATHEMATICAL THEOLOGY

RATIONALITY, as an attribute of man, enters the argument at two points. It is because we are rational, and can get the hang of Gödel-type arguments, that we can be sure of our always being able to produce a suitable particular argument to fault any physical system the physical determinist thinks up—rationality gives us the last laugh. But more fundamentally still, it is because we are rational that we can see the Gödelian formula to be true even though it cannot be proved-in-the-logistic-calculus-*L*. We are continually drawing the contrast between what physical systems cannot do and what men, being rational self-conscious agents, can do. Given a particular physical system, we construct that particular Gödelian formula which even the physical determinist, according to his own principles, has to admit the physical system cannot produce as true; and then we hope that the physical determinist, as a man, a rational self-conscious agent, will see that he can do better and that this *sort* of argument will always apply against any sort of physical determinism he espouses. We have on the one hand formal, precise, rigorous arguments, which are incontrovertible but intricate and nearly unintelligible to the layman: and we have on the other hand intuitive but vague attempts to capture what is essential to being a man, a rational self-conscious agent, a person or a self, attempts that are resistant to exact definition but none the less widely used and well understood. But they can be resisted and they can be misunderstood, and a natural line of defence for the physical determinist is to refuse to see the force of some of the informal arguments we have used, and to criticize these as uncompelling or invalid.

One criticism is not made. Nobody doubts that Gödel's proof is valid. It has been scrutinised repeatedly by mathematicians, and all competent critics are satisfied that it is completely rigorous. Nor do many doubt that suitable variants of the Gödelian type of argument could be devised for any logistic calculus corresponding to a determinist physical system. Some philosophers, however, object to the form in which I have cited the theorem.[1] The word 'true' does not occur in the formal proof because truth, as we have seen,[2] cannot be adequately formalised. All the formal proof shows is that granted certain conditions of consistency, the logistic calculus L is incomplete, because it contains a well-formed formula which is unprovable-in-the-logistic-calculus-L and whose negation is unprovable-in-the-logistic-calculus-L. Our argument, that the Gödelian formula, although unprovable-in-the-logistic-calculus-L, is nonetheless true, is essentially an informal argument, containing as it does the unformalised notion of truth. And therefore it is open to objection by formal-minded philosophers. And if they object, we cannot refute them. For to refute them would be to *prove*—prove formally—that the Gödelian formula was true, and the whole nerve of the argument is that we cannot prove it formally within the given logistic calculus L. One just has to step outside the system and "see" that it is true—that it "stands to reason" that it is true. But we cannot make people see reason or take a step they do not want to take, unless we have a formal proof within a system they have accepted. We cannot define truth. Truth is not simply provability-in-a-given-logistic-calculus—Gödel's theorem shows this. But if a tough-minded philosopher asks "If truth is not provability-in-a-given system what is it?" I cannot answer him. I think I know what truth is, but I know I cannot tell anybody else exactly what it is. I can recognise—subject to many mistakes, errors and oversights—various propositions, formulae, statements and theories, as true, or come to that conclusion after due consideration. In particular cases I can explain why, and often hope to convince somebody else as well. But I cannot produce a formula which will cover all cases, or frame an instruction which somebody else could apply mechanically in all cases. I can communicate the idea to him, but he will need, on occasion, to use his own *nous* and make up his mind for himself. If it were not so, I doubt if we could regard anybody else as being any*body else*; a listener I could completely instruct in all the truth would

---

[1] L. Goddard, "'True' and 'Provable'", *Mind*, LXVII, 1958, pp. 13–31; Richard Butrick, "The Gödel Formula: some Reservations", *Mind*, LXXIV, 1965, pp. 411–414.

[2] Section 24, pp. 125–126.

not seem to have a mind (be any*body* rather than any*thing*) independently of me (be *else*, or *other than* me). Some degree of intellectual autonomy is a necessary condition of being a rational agent. And therefore truth cannot be precisely defined. We therefore cannot make people see that the Gödelian formula is true, and at this point there is an ineliminable appeal to intuition. The reader must examine Gödel's argument and decide for himself whether the Gödelian formula really is, as I allege, true, according to an intuitive notion of truth, which is, I believe, understood, but which cannot be defined in precise and formal terms.[1] It is Freedom's debt to Truth.

Formalists, therefore, eschew the notion of truth, and the debate with them must be carried on by means of Gödel's second theorem rather than his first with the concept of consistency as the crucial one.[2] It is a natural shift. If we were faced with a recalcitrant sceptic who refused to see that the Gödelian formula was true, we might try to formalise Gödel's own argument. After all, I have claimed that it is completely rigorous, and surely such a claim could not be sustained unless we could, step by step, force a recalcitrant reasoner to acknowledge the cogency of the argument. And to do this, would be to formalise it. Therefore, surely, we *must* be able to *prove* the truth of the Gödelian formula—although, if we could, it would have the embarrassing consequence of proving that it was not, as it claimed itself, unprovable, and therefore of proving it to be itself false. However, when we come to make the attempt, we find that what we can formally prove in a logistic calculus L is *not* that

$$G \text{ is true,}$$

but that,

if L is consistent, then G is unprovable-in-L.

If we could prove to our recalcitrant reasoner that L was consistent, then he would have to admit that G was unprovable-in-L,

[1] See J. R. Lucas, "True", *Philosophy*, XLIV, 1969, pp. 175–186.

[2] For example, Hilary Putnam, "Minds and Machines", in Sydney Hook, ed., *Dimensions of Mind*, New York, 1960 and 1961, p. 142 of Collier edition; reprinted in Alan Ross Anderson, ed., *Minds and Machines*, Prentice-Hall, 1964, p. 77; Hartley Rogers, *Theory of Recursive Functions and Effective Computability*, vol. I, Massachusetts Institute of Technology (mimeographed), 1957, pp. 152ff.; Paul Benacerraf, "God, the Devil, and Gödel", *The Monist*, **51**, 1967, pp. 9–32; and J. J. C. Smart, *Between Science and Philosophy*, New York, 1968, pp. 317–322.

and, if he had any use for the word 'true', that it was true that G was unprovable-in-L, or simply that G was true. But, as Gödel argued in his second theorem—a corollary of his first—, it is impossible to prove in a consistent logistic calculus that that logistic calculus is itself consistent. For, as we can now see quite easily, if we had a proof-in-L that L was itself consistent, then, by *Modus Ponens*, we should have a *proof-in-L* that G was unprovable-in-L. Thus we should have both proved-in-L that G was unprovable-in-L, and at the same time produced a proof-in-L of G; and hence an inconsistency. Thus we cannot prove-in-L that L is itself consistent. And therefore the recalcitrant reasoner may put it to the question and ask what warrant we have for assuming consistency, in the absence of proof.

The answer is provided by the physical determinist himself, thanks to the dialectical structure of the argument. He is claiming that his physical description describes a human being. But if it does, then the logistic calculus that represents human reasoning must be consistent; else the claim that the description is a plausible one fails at the outset. The physical determinist claims that he can, in principle at least, produce a completely adequate description of any given human being in purely physical terms. If so, to any features characteristic of human beings, there must correspond features with the same characteristics in the physical system. But human reasoning is consistent.[1] Therefore, the logistic calculus that corresponds to it in the alleged physical description of a particular human being must be consistent too. We obtain the premiss we need, that L is consistent, from the physical determinist's own claim. The dialectical structure of the argument entitles us to assume what we cannot directly prove. The argument is a dialectical *reductio ad absurdum*. We take certain premisses the physical determinist supplies, and show that, in virtue of Gödel's theorem, they lead to a contradiction; from which we argue that the thesis of physical determinism itself is the one to be rejected.

The physical determinist may seek to avoid refutation in a number of ways. He may seek to jettison some other premiss— for example, that human reasoning is consistent—or he may refuse to "play the game" by not conceding premisses which he actually holds, or not conceding them in the form required. In so

[1] See further below, p. 161.

far as the rules of discussion are not formalised, it is possible not to play the two-person argument game without transgressing any formal rule, and therefore without being open to formal refutation. In mathematics the Intuitionists refuse to play the game as classical mathematicians understand it, without being guilty of any inconsistency according to their own terms of reference.[1] In the same way a highly recalcitrant reasoner might hope to avoid having to abandon physical determinism by not granting what he does in fact believe to be true, or by not accepting some valid but as yet unformalised inference. Against such a position we can either continue to argue informally, appealing as it were to the physical determinist's better (*i.e.* more rational) nature, and relying on the fact that he is, despite his protests, really a man, and capable of informal ratiocination: or we may recast our dialectical arguments into monologous form, in which case they will appear as various sorts of *reductio ad absurdum*, revealing the price in absurdity, if not formal inconsistency, of the various positions the physical determinist is forced back upon.

The physical determinist may refuse to *say* that the logistic calculus L is consistent, although privately believing that it is. He produces a specification of a physical system which he maintains is equivalent to me, but professes not to know whether it is consistent or not. After all, the word 'consistent' does not apply to physical systems as such, but only to logistic calculi.[2] The question can easily be made out to be meaningless; or if allowed to be meaningful, unanswerable on account of the enormous complexity involved. The physical determinist cannot afford, however, to be altogether agnostic about his physical system, if he wants us to believe both that it is a physical system and that it is equivalent to some particular man. He must know rather a lot about it in order to have convinced himself that it was capable of doing all that the man could. In particular, he must know what the logistic calculus is that characterizes the physical system's intellectual output—if he had not assured himself that the physical system could operate the principle of mathematical induction, his claim would be a highly unconvincing one. Hence

[1] See more fully, J. R. Lucas, "Not 'Therefore' but 'But'", *The Philosophical Quarterly*, **16**, 1966, pp. 301–307.

[2] It is easy to be confused because a logistic calculus is often called a formal system. See above, Section 17, pp. 91–92.

we can ask the physical determinist quite a number of questions about the "intellectual powers" of his physical system and expect an answer, if his claim that the physical system is equivalent to a certain man is ever to get off the ground. In particular, we can construct the Gödelian formula and ask the physical determinist whether the physical system can produce that as true or not. If it can, it is inconsistent, and can prove anything, and produce as true any proposition whatever, and therefore is unlike a man: if it cannot, it is consistent, and *therefore* the *man* can assert, unconditionally, its truth, and thus show himself different from the physical system in question.

Three ploys are open to physical determinist to avoid having to concede consistency *via* the unprovability-in-the-logistic-calculus-*L* of the Gödelian formula of *L*. He may try to avoid exposing his Achilles' heel by not standing four-square in his position: he may hope that the fantastic complexity of the logistic calculus will prevent its Gödelian formula from ever being constructed or ever being seen by any mortal man to be true: or finally he may plead that ignorance on the Gödelian question is not a failing but a positive mathematical duty for a mere physical system like himself. None of these moves will in the event provide an escape-route, but none can be dismissed out of hand.

Since the Gödelian formula depends on, among other things, the particular logistic calculus in question, the determinist could avoid refutation by not specifying which logistic calculus represented on his view the thinking of a particular man, simply maintaining that the man was *a* physical system whose working was equivalent to *a* logistic calculus, and leave it at that.

If given a black box and told not to peek inside, then what reason is there to suppose that Lucas or I can determine its program by watching its output. But I must be able to determine its program (if this makes sense) if I am to carry out Gödel's argument in connection with it. . . . If the machine is not designated in such a way that there is an effective procedure for recovering the machine's program from the designation, one may well know that one is presented with a machine but yet be unable to do anything about finding the Gödel sentence for it. The problem becomes even more intractable if one supposes the machine to be oneself—for in that case there may be no way of discovering a relevant index—of finding out one's own program.[1]

[1] P. Benacerraf, "God, The Devil, and Gödel", *The Monist*, 1967, p. 28.

But how do we know that the black box is a physical system? If we are not to look inside, the only way we could know is if we are told by somebody else—the determinist who claims that the black box is both a physical system and has an output equivalent to the intellectual output of a particular man. But if he is to be certain that a particular black box is equivalent to a particular man, he must have acquainted himself with the design of the black box very thoroughly, in which case he will know which logistic calculus it embodies, and even if he keeps this information to himself in order not to be refuted, he will himself be able to see what formula is the Gödelian one, which the black box could not, and the man could, produce as true. The very stratagem employed to ward off defeat shows that even the determinist knows his position is untenable. The position becomes not so much untenable as vacuous if the "machine" is presented not as a black box but as the man himself: for then, in the absence of a specific description of the working of the alleged machine, what is being claimed when it is said that the man is a machine? If we cannot say what sort of machine but only that it is *that* machine, pointing to the man, our hearers will conclude that we are giving a new sense to the word 'machine' rather than making a substantial claim. It is the specification which gives content to the claim, and if no specification is possible, no real claim is being made.

It might be protested that we often make claims without being able to be completely specific. We have the indefinite article for that very purpose. Only a mathematical intuitionist would maintain that we should never use the indefinite article unless we could equally well have used the definite article together with an identifying description. Could not the determinist's thesis be like Brower's Fixed-Point Theorem? Could we not affirm that this particular man was equivalent to a logistic calculus, although we do not know which, in just the same way as we affirm that this particular transformation over a closed portion of a plane leaves a point unaltered, although we do not know which? The answer is No. The cases are not alike. If at some later time a mathematician were to produce a constructive proof, which not only entitled us to say that there was a point unaltered by the transformation, but enabled us to say what, for each transformation, it must be, then, far from being embarrassed by the discovery, we

should welcome it, as vindicating Brower's original insight even
to his later self. But the determinist would be floored, not
vindicated, by such a discovery. Benacerraf's determinist, therefore, is not merely being modest, nor is he simply playing with his
cards close to his chest; rather, he is being ω-inconsistent.[1] He is
claiming that the man is a physical system although for every
particular system he could be we can show that he is not that one.
It is not simply that, as Benacerraf suggests, "*I am indeed a*

[1] ω-consistency is a slightly stronger condition than simple consistency.
It rules out the further possibility that the logistic calculus might contain
both $(\exists x)F(x)$ *and* $\sim F(0)$, $\sim F(1)$, $\sim F(2)$, . . ., *etc.* Such a possibility need
not yield a simple inconsistency, because the logistic calculus might be so
limited that although we could prove $\sim F(n)$ for *each n*, we could not
prove the formula expressing the generalisation $(x) \sim F(x)$, which would
be the negation of $(\exists x)F(x)$. In such a logistic calculus it would be possible
to have true the negation of the Gödelian formula—*i.e.* $(\exists x)F(x)$, where
$F(x)$ meant that x was the Gödel number of a proof of the Gödelian
formula—but not have $F(n)$ true for any particular n—*i.e.* without its
being true for any particular number that it is the Gödel number of a
proof of the Gödelian formula. We thus could claim that the Gödelian
formula was untrue without having to concede that a particular proof
could be produced which would force us to admit that it was true. Thus
the third possibility envisaged in Section 24 on pp. 127–128, that the
Gödelian formula was untrue but provable-in-the-logistic-calculus-*L*
would hold in so far as we were using the formal analogue of 'provable'
in a Pickwickian sense, where being 'provable' was consistent with there
being no actual proof. Indeed, so far as Gödel's original proof goes, there
could be an ω-inconsistent calculus in which the negation of the Gödelian
formula might be not only true, but provable. There could be a logistic
calculus in which we could actually produce a formal proof of the negation
of the Gödelian formula, although we could also prove-in-that-logistic-
calculus for every particular number that it was not the Gödel number of
the required proof. We should not have a proof-in-the-logistic-calculus of
a formal inconsistency, although we should regard it as being pretty well
inconsistent both to say that there was a proof, and to deny of each
possible proof that it was the proof in question. For the sake of exactitude
we distinguish this sort of inconsistency from the simple one of a direct
contradiction where we assert both p and $\sim p$: but for our purposes, an
ω-inconsistent logistic calculus would be as implausible a representation
of human thinking as a fully inconsistent one. Although in his original
proof Gödel needed the assumption of ω-consistency in order to show
that the negation of the Gödelian formula was unprovable-in-the-system,
J. Barkley Rosser, "Extensions of some theorems of Gödel and Church",
Journal of Symbolic Logic, I, 1936, pp. 87–91, has shown that simple
consistency is enough.

Turing machine but one with such a complex machine table (program) that I cannot ascertain what it is":[1] my ignorance is more necessary than that, and more fatal to his thesis. The only way I can be absolutely sure of not knowing that I am any particular machine (or physical system *L*), is by not being any machine (or physical system) whatever.

A second objection[2] may be based on complexity: with a sufficiently complex description of a physical system it might be well-nigh impossible for any human being to figure out what was its Gödelian formula, or to *see* that it was true. A description which could claim, with any plausibility, to describe a human being would be fantastically complex. Might it not be that with logistic calculi of this complexity the limit of the human mathematician's computing power was reached? After all, men are mortal, and can achieve only a limited degree of understanding in their seventy odd years. But the shortness of life is not decisive. Other mathematicians could come to the aid of the one whom the physical determinist claimed to have completely described, and help him find out the Gödelian formula of the logistic calculus generated by the description, and see that it was true. More generally, considerations of finitude are not relevant, because we are questioning whether *in principle* a human being could be, as the physical determinists allege, completely described in purely physical terms. The thesis is an ideal one—in principle, not in practice—and therefore must be considered under ideal conditions. Can the ideal rational being be completely described by an ideal physical description? To which the argument from human finitude is not relevant.

The third objection is based on the fact that the question whether or not the Gödelian formula of a logistic calculus *L* can be proved-in-the-logistic-calculus-*L* is one which itself cannot be answered in the logistic calculus *L*. Turing machines are embarrassed, naturally enough, by this question about their own powers.[3] If we are to ask the question, we must ask it of the physical determinist, not the physical system itself. We are

[1] *op. cit.* p. 29.

[2] Put forward by Mr. M. J. Lockwood, of Exeter College, Oxford, in a letter.

[3] See, for example, Martin Davis, *Computability and Unsolvability*, New York, 1958, Preface, p. vii.

assuming, that is, that the determinist is different from what is being said to be determined, and that assumption may be put in question. It could be that the physical determinist was not only a physical system but the very same physical system that he had specified. In which case he would indeed be unable to say whether it could produce the Gödelian formula as true or not. His agnosticism would be a logically necessary one, and no fault of his, nor sign of falsity of his thesis. But we have no reason to suppose that the same logistic calculus represents everybody's intellectual output. And, more fundamentally, it is again an ideal thesis which is being considered. The question is an askable one, and therefore one we can press, in principle if not in practice. So long as there is, or could be, any person or other rational being in the universe—even myself—who does, or might, maintain that I am equivalent to a physical system, I can consider what answer would have to be given to a Gödelian question, to reveal whether the logistic calculus embodied in the physical system is consistent or not, and, either way, to show that physical determinism is false.

Ignorance is of no avail when impaled on the horns of a dilemma, and the physical determinist is faced with a dilemma. Behind the tricksy question about the Gödelian formula lies the substantial issue of consistency. Either the logistic calculus is inconsistent, or it is consistent. If it is inconsistent, it is degenerate, not a proper logistic calculus at all, and not a plausible candidate for being any sort of description of me or any other man. Only if it is consistent, and represented as such, is it even a candidate; and then, being consistent and being acknowledged as consistent, I can out-Gödel it. Either way, it cannot be a plausible description of a man. And therefore, even if we do not in fact know whether a particular logistic calculus is consistent or not, we can be certain that it is not an adequate representation of the whole of a man's thinking.

In the propositional calculus, disjunction can be defined in terms of implication and negation, and Putnam and Benacerraf seek to evade the dilemma by representing it as a conditional implication in which the antecedent can never be asserted as an independent premiss in the form required. Instead of the dilemma: Either the logistic calculus L is inconsistent or the Gödelian formula of L both can be seen to be true by me and is unprovable-in-the-logistic-calculus-L, Putnam suggests that the argument should be put in the following five propositions:

(1) If L is inconsistent, then $L \neq$ me
(2) See$_I$ (If L is consistent, then G)

(3) If L is consistent, then See$_I(G)$
(4) If L is consistent, then $\sim$ See$_L(G)$
(5) If L is consistent, then $L \neq$ me

where See$_I$ (....) means 'I can see it to be true that ....' See$_L$ (....) means 'It can be proved in L that ....', and G is the Gödelian formula of L. Putnam objects that the third proposition does not follow from the second, and that therefore the whole proof-sequence is invalid. And since I have given no formal rules for the use of 'I can see it to be true that ....', and indeed, have said that such a notion cannot be completely formalised,[1] his attack seems strong.

If proposition (3) does not follow from proposition (2), then it should be possible to affirm both (2) and the negation of (3), namely

(3̄) Although L is consistent, $\sim$ See$_I(G)$.

I should have to affirm both that I could see that if L is consistent, then G, and that Although L is consistent, I cannot see that G is true. And this is absurd. All that I can say, in conjunction with (2) is

(3̄)* Although L may be consistent, $\sim$ See$_I(G)$.

What gives Putnam's argument its plausibility is that (3̄) can be affirmed, together with (2), by some third person. Putnam can say of Lucas, both that Lucas can see that If L is consistent, then G, and that Although L is consistent, Lucas (who is not entitled to assume that it is) cannot see that G is true (because although L is consistent, since Lucas is not entitled to assume that it is, he cannot use it as a premiss from which to conclude that G is true). But I cannot say the same of myself. The nearest thing to it that I can say is that Although L *may be* consistent, I (who am not entitled to assume that it is) cannot see that G is true (because even if L is consistent, I am not entitled to assume that it is). Moods and persons are closely interlocked here. In changing from the third to the first person, one must also change the categorical

[1] Section 24, pp. 125–126.

indicative to a hypothetical subjunctive. Else the concession made in the 'although' clause belies the rider in brackets, which is essential for Putnam's conclusion: if I am not entitled to assume that L is consistent, I must not assume that it *is*—though I may assume that it may be. *If* I am making the categorical assumption expressed by the clause 'Although L *is* consistent' *then* I *can* see that G is true, in virtue of what I can see in (2). Once I have accepted (2), I cannot make the concession that L is consistent and deny that I can see that G is true; although somebody else could make the concession that L is consistent without having to concede that I, a different person, could therefore see that G was true. It is therefore impossible for me to deny Putnam's proposition (3) while affirming his proposition (2), and hence the argument is valid, and his objection fails.

The key to Putnam's defence is that the physical determinist, although privately believing L to be consistent—else, as admitted in (1), it would not be equivalent to me—keeps this opinion to himself, and does not admit it to me, so as to deprive me of the premiss I need if I am to draw the conclusion that G is true. And the reason why such a manoeuvre fails is that, while in a dialogue it may merely lead to a stalemate, if I internalise both sides of the argument—if I am arguing not with somebody else but with my own *alter ego*—it makes my position untenable. I reduce myself to absurdity in the effort to see that I cannot see what I can see. For if I can see it to be true that If L is consistent, then G, I can also see it to be true that If L is consistent, I can see it to be true that G. For I can *understand* Gödel's theorem. I can reflect on it, and see how, granted consistency, I can follow through the argument and come myself to see the truth of the Gödelian formula. Hence I can see it to be true that If L is consistent, I can see it to be true that G; or more formally,

$$(3)' \quad \text{See}_I \text{ (If } L \text{ is consistent, then See}_I(G)).$$

If we place a See_I before propositions (1), (3), (4) and (5), we have a valid argument which I should have to accept if I were a physical determinist, leading by a dilemma to a *reductio ad absurdum*. And so, granted the premisses, and in particular (1), that an inconsistent L cannot represent human reasoning, it follows that physical determinism must be false.

But is human reasoning consistent? And even if it is, can we assert it? After all, men are sometimes inconsistent. Certainly women are, and politicians; and even male non-politicians contradict themselves on occasion; and a single inconsistency is enough to make a logistic calculus inconsistent. The very fact that we often assert our consistency, often indeed with vehemence, has been taken by some philosophers as evidence, in view of Gödel's second theorem, of our actual inconsistency. Perhaps after all we are inconsistent, in which case the whole Gödelian argument ceases to apply.

The fact that we are all sometimes inconsistent cannot be gainsaid, but from this it does not follow that we are tantamount to inconsistent logistic calculi. Our inconsistencies are mistakes rather than set policies. They correspond to the occasional malfunctioning of a system, not its normal scheme of operations. Witness to this that we eschew inconsistencies when we recognise them for what they are. If we really were inconsistent systems, we should remain content with our inconsistencies, and would happily affirm both halves of a contradiction. Moreover, we would be prepared to say absolutely anything—which we are not. It is easily shown[1] that in an inconsistent logistic calculus everything is provable, and the requirement of consistency turns out to be just that not everything can be proved in it—it is not the case that "anything goes". This surely is a characteristic of the mental operations of human beings: they are selective: they do discriminate between favoured—true—and unfavoured—false—statements: when a person is prepared to say anything, and is prepared to contradict himself without any qualm or repugnance, then he is adjudged to have "lost his mind". Human beings, although not perfectly consistent, are not so much inconsistent as fallible.

A fallible but self-correcting system would still be subject to Gödel's results. Only a fundamentally inconsistent system would escape. Could we have a fundamentally inconsistent, but at the same time self-correcting system, which both would be free of Gödel's results and yet would not be trivial and entirely unlike a human being? A system with a rather *recherché* inconsistency in it, so that for all normal purposes it was consistent, but when presented with the Gödelian sentence was able to prove it?

[1] See, *e.g.*, Alonzo Church, *Introduction to Mathematical Logic*, Princeton, 1956, Vol. I, Section 17, p. 108.

There are all sorts of ways in which undesirable proofs might be obviated. We might have a rule that whenever we have proved p and not-p, we examine their proofs and reject the longer. Or we might arrange the axioms and rules of inference in a certain order, and when a proof leading to an inconsistency is proffered, see what axioms and rules are required for it, and reject that axiom or rule which comes last in the ordering. In some such way as this we could have an inconsistent system, with a stop-rule, so that the inconsistency was never allowed to come out in the form of an inconsistent formula.

The suggestion at first sight seems attractive: yet there is something deeply wrong. Even though we might preserve the façade of consistency by having a rule that whenever two incon-sistent formulae appeared we were to reject the one with the longer proof, yet such a rule would be repugnant in our logical sense. Even the less arbitrary suggestions are too arbitrary. No longer does the calculus operate with certain definite rules of inference on certain definite formulae. Instead, the rules apply, the axioms are true, provided . . . provided we do not happen to find it inconvenient. We no longer know where we stand. One application of the rule of *Modus Ponens* may be accepted while another is rejected: on one occasion an axiom may be true, on another apparently false. The calculus will have ceased to be a formal logistic calculus, and the description of the physical system will barely qualify as a description of a human being with a mind. For it will be far from resembling the mind in its operations: the mind does indeed try out dubious axioms and rules of inference; but if they are found to lead to contradiction, they are rejected altogether. We try out axioms and rules of inference provisionally—true: but we do not keep them, once they are found to lead to contradictions. We may seek to replace them with others, we may feel that our formalisation is at fault, and that though some axiom or rule of inference of this sort is required, we have not been able to formulate it quite correctly: but we do not retain the faulty formulations without modification, merely with the proviso that when the argument leads to a con-tradiction we refuse to follow it. To do this would be utterly irrational. We should be in the position that on some occasions when supplied with the premisses of a *Modus Ponens*, say, we applied the rule and allowed the conclusion, and on other occasions we refused to apply the rule, and disallowed the conclusion. A person who did this without being able to give a good reason for so doing, would be accounted arbitrary and irrational. It is part of the concept of "arguments" or "reasons" that they are in some sense general and universal: that if *Modus Ponens* is a valid method of arguing when I am establishing a desired conclusion, it is a valid method also when you, my opponent, are establishing a conclusion I do not want to accept. We cannot pick and choose the times when a form of argument is to be valid; not if we are to be reasonable. It is of course true, that with our informal arguments, which are not fully formalised, we do distinguish between arguments which are at first sight similar, adding further reasons why they are nonetheless not really similar: and it might be maintained that this feature should appear in the physical determinist's description of a human being. But the physical determinist's description is *not* informal. It necessarily represents reasoning by a formal logistic calculus. There must be formal rules saying when a given type of inference is permissible or not. And it would not be enough merely to forbid simply those inferences which would lead to a contradiction. The mere avoidance of contradiction, if it is a reason at all for disallowing an inference, is too good a reason. We do not lay it to a man's credit that he avoids contradiction merely by refusing to accept those arguments which would lead him to it, for no other reason than that otherwise he would be led to it. Special pleading rather than sound argument is the name for that type of reasoning. No credit accrues to a man who, clever enough to see a few moves of argument ahead, avoids being brought to acknowledge his own inconsistency by stonewalling as soon as he sees where the argument will end. Rather, we account him inconsistent too, not, in his case, because he affirmed and denied the same proposition, but because he used and refused to use the same rule of inference. A stop-rule on actually enunciating an inconsistency is not enough to save an inconsistent system from being called inconsistent.

The possibility yet remains that we are inconsistent, and there is no stop-rule, but the inconsistency is so *recherché* that it has never turned up. After all, *naïve* set-theory, which was deeply embedded in common-sense ways of thinking did turn out to be inconsistent.[1] Can we be sure that a similar fate is not in store for

[1] See above, Section 22, pp. 117–119.

simple arithmetic too? In a sense we cannot, in spite of our great feeling of certitude that our logistic calculus of whole numbers which can be added and multiplied together is never going to prove inconsistent. It is just conceivable we might find we had formalised it incorrectly If we had, we should try and formulate anew our intuitive concept of a number, as we have our intuitive concept of a set. If we did this, we should of course recast our logistic calculus: our present axioms and rules of inference would be utterly rejected: there would be no question of our using and not using them in an "inconsistent" fashion. We should, once we had recast the logistic calculus, be in the same position as we are now, possessed of a logistic calculus believed to be consistent, but not provably so. But then could there not be some other inconsistency? It is indeed a possibility. But again no inconsistency once detected will be tolerated. We shall modify our axioms or rules of inference in a way which will appear reasonable, but which cannot be anticipated or prescribed in advance by any antecedently specified formal rule. We are determined not to be inconsistent, and are resolved to root out inconsistency, should any appear. Thus, although we can never be completely certain or completely free of the risk of having to think out our mathematics again, the ultimate position must be one of two: either we have a logistic calculus of simple arithmetic which to the best of our knowledge and belief is consistent; or there is no such logistic calculus possible. In the former case we are in the same position as at present: in the latter, if we find that no system containing simple arithmetic can be free of contradictions, we shall have to abandon not merely the whole of mathematics and the mathematical sciences, but the whole of thought.

It may still be maintained that although a human being must in this sense assume, he cannot properly affirm, his own consistency without thereby belying his words. We may be consistent; indeed we have every reason to hope that we are: but a necessary modesty forbids us from saying so. Yet this is not quite what Gödel's second theorem states. Gödel has shown that in a consistent logistic calculus a formula stating the consistency of the logistic calculus cannot be proved *in that logistic calculus*. It follows that any instance of a physical description cannot, if its reasoning processes can be represented by a consistent logistic calculus, produce as true a statement of its own consistency: and hence that a human being, *if he really could be completely described in physical terms*, could not reach the conclusion that he was consistent. But no such conclusion follows for a human being who cannot be completely described in physical terms. All that Gödel has proved is that a human being cannot produce a formal proof of the consistency of a logistic calculus inside the calculus itself: but there is not objection to going outside the logistic calculus and no objection to producing informal arguments for the consistency either of a logistic calculus or of something less formal and less systematized. Such informal arguments will not be able to be completely formalised: but then the whole tenor of Gödel's results is that we ought not to ask, and cannot obtain, complete formalisation.[1] And although it would have been nice if we could have obtained them, since completely formalised arguments are more coercive than informal ones, yet since we cannot have all our arguments cast into that form we must not hold it against informal arguments that they are informal or regard them all as utterly worthless. It therefore seems to me both proper and reasonable to assert one's own consistency: proper, because although purely physical systems, as we might have expected, are unable to reflect fully on their own performance and powers, yet to be able to be self-conscious in this way is just what we expect of conscious human beings: and reasonable, for the reasons given. Not only can we fairly say simply that we *know* we are consistent, apart from our mistakes, but we must in any case *assume* that we are, if thought is to be possible at all. Moreover we are selective: we will not, as inconsistent physical systems would, say anything and everything whatsoever: and finally we can, in a sense, *decide* to be consistent, in the sense that we can resolve not to tolerate inconsistencies in our thinking and speaking, and to eliminate them, if ever they should appear, by withdrawing and cancelling one limb of the contradiction.

If we are consistent and can say that we are, it follows without more ado from Gödel's second theorem that we cannot be completely described as physical systems instantiating some logistic calculus. But, in so far as we are rational self-conscious agents, both conditions are satisfied. Under that description "there are

[1] See more fully, C. T. K. Chari, "Further Comments on Minds, Machines and Gödel", *Philosophy*, XXXVIII, 1963, pp. 175–178.

distinctive attributes which enable a human being to transcend this last limitation [*i.e.* of Gödel's second theorem] and assert his own consistency while still remaining consistent".[1] It is both necessary for a rational self-conscious agent to be consistent and possible for him to say that he is, and therefore he cannot be completely explained in physical terms. There are, we have seen, reasons why a rational agent must be consistent. And they are reasons which a rational self-conscious agent can appreciate and himself accept. It is rational for a rational agent to believe in his own rationality, and hence in his own consistency, and if it is rational for him to believe in it, it is permissible for him to make a profession of his faith and affirm that he is consistent, defending it both as a necessary presupposition of thought, the only assumption on which further thought is possible, and as an act of will, a decision he has made, the decision to be consistent, to discipline his thinking, not to allow himself to affirm anything whatever, but to draw some distinction between truth and falsehood. It is, in the language of mathematical theology, a profession of faith. No formal proof is possible: but the alternative is self-stultifying. If, ultimately, I were an inconsistent physical system, I could not ever distinguish between those propositions which were true and worthy to be believed and those which were false and meet to be rejected: and I could not believe that I might not be consistent without abandoning my conviction that there was a distinction between truth and falsehood which I ought always to endeavour to observe in my own thinking, with some hope of occasional success. And so, although the possibility of my being essentially inconsistent cannot be ruled out by purely formal arguments and is perhaps just conceivable,[2] it is a position of complete conceptual nihilism, and one which I, like any rational agent, am reasonably reluctant to adopt.

[1] Hartley Rogers, *Theory of Recursive Functions and Effective Computability*, Vol. I, Massachusetts Institute of Technology (mimeographed), 1957, p. 154.
[2] As on p. 161 above.

29

REFLECTIONS ON THE GÖDELIAN ARGUMENT

WE might almost have expected Gödel's theorem to distinguish self-conscious beings from inanimate objects. The essence of the Gödelian formula is that it is self-referring. It says that "This formula is unprovable-in-the-logistic-calculus". When carried over to a physical description, the formula is specified in terms which depend on the particular physical description in question. The system as described is being asked a question about its own processes. We are asking it to be self-conscious, and say what things it can and cannot do. Such questions notoriously lead to paradox. At one's first and simplest attempts to philosophize, one becomes entangled in questions of whether when one knows something one knows that one knows it; and what, when one is thinking of oneself, is being thought about, and what is doing the thinking. After one has been puzzled and bruised by this problem for a long time, one learns not to press these questions: the concept of a conscious being is, implicitly, realised to be different from that of an unconscious object. In saying that a conscious being knows something, we are saying not only that he knows it, but that he knows that he knows it, and that he knows that he knows that he knows it, and so on, as long as we care to pose the question: there is, we recognise, an infinity here, but it is not an infinite regress in the bad sense, for it is the questions that peter out, as being pointless, rather than the answers. The questions are felt to be pointless because the concept contains within itself the idea of being able to go on answering such questions indefinitely. Although conscious beings have the power of going on, we do not wish to exhibit this simply as a succession of tasks they are able to perform, nor do we see the mind as an infinite sequence of selves and super-selves and super-super-selves. Rather, we insist that a conscious being is a unity, and though we talk about parts of the mind, we do so only as a metaphor, and will not allow it to be taken literally. The paradoxes of consciousness arise because a conscious being can be aware of itself, as well as of other things, and yet cannot really be construed as being divisible into parts. It means that a conscious being can deal with Gödelian questions in a way in which a physical system cannot, because a conscious being can both consider itself and its performance and yet not be other than that which did the performance. A physical system can be made in a manner of speaking to "consider" its own performance, but it cannot take this "into account" without thereby becoming different. But it is inherent in our idea of a conscious mind that it can reflect upon itself and criticize its own performances, without thereby becoming different. Gödel's theorem only enables us to express in mathematical terms what we have always known about a man's own awareness of himself.

We know that we are conscious. We know that we are reasonable, although only imperfectly so. Because we are aware of ourselves, and capable of reflecting upon our own potentialities and performances without thereby becoming different beings from what we were, any description which claims to be a complete description of a human being must offer a description of similar self-reflective processes and similar reasoning ones; else it is confessedly incomplete. But any description of human beings and human activity which is entirely rule-governed and admits of only regularity explanations is sufficiently rule-governed to constitute a formal logistic calculus, and is open to Gödel-type arguments. What exact form we cannot say in advance, but we can be sure that as soon as the physical determinist has made his claim sufficiently specific for it to be a definite one and to have implications for human freedom and responsibility, we shall be able to devise a Gödelian formula which will be the Achilles' heel of his description. And by concentrating on this formula we shall be able to assure ourselves of what we already believed, namely that the description was only an incomplete one of the particular human being in question.

Our argument is thus, at bottom, one of conceptual analysis rather than mathematical discovery. It is not that some very *recherché* result in pure mathematics had proved that the world, as a matter of contingent fact, is undetermined. It is, rather, that Gödel's theorem enables us to crystallize out our intuitive notions and intimations of freedom in such a way that we can be sure that they apply to any form of physical determinism, however it may be articulated. Gödel's theorem provides a spanner rather than a premiss. It enables us to formulate the objection we felt to the determinist's maintaining that what he said was true, in spite of his being determined, in a way which is not liable to the charge of meaninglessness that can be made against most self-referential arguments. And because Gödel's theorem is an entirely formal result it applies to all reductive analyses of human behaviour in terms of rule-bound descriptions and regularity explanations, in whatever form they are put forward. They, just because they are rule-bound, cannot cope with the Gödelian formula: whereas we, since we are not, can.

We know that we are conscious. We know that we are reasonable, although only imperfectly so. Any attempt to make out that, really speaking, we are merely machines, merely physical systems, must fail. We have always apprehended this. Many people have always rejected any reductive analysis which purported to explain away human behaviour in entirely non-human terms or to describe human beings completely in purely thing-like categories. But the arguments have been difficult to formulate, difficult to grapple with. The merit of Gödel's theorem is that it enables us to do just that, and provides—to change the metaphor —a lens, whereby we can get the issues into focus, and see exactly how the argument goes, and know clearly what we had always dimly believed.

§30

CONSEQUENCES

THE consequences of the Gödelian argument are great. The argument applies to any form of physical determinism that is sufficiently definite to pose any threat to freedom. Although we naturally think of some Newtonian sort of physical determinism, the argument would apply equally to a version of quantum mechanics into which hidden parameters had, *per impossibile*, been introduced.[1] Any claim to reduce, explain, or give a complete description of, human beings and human action will stand refuted, provided only that the reduction, explanation or description is in terms of regularities alone. But only such reductions, explanations and descriptions need alarm us. For only these threaten us with iron rules, ineluctable laws, inevitable necessities. Other sorts of explanation remain possible: indeed, even regularity explanations are entirely all right, so long as they do not claim to be complete.[2]

It may be that the human organism is like a quantum mechanical system, *any* observable feature of which may be measured and determined precisely, but not all of them. With sufficient care, and perhaps with sufficient brutality, we can "put" any question we can express in physical terms to a human organism, and may be able to extract an adequately precise answer; but not all questions together. This may be so. We do not know. What we do know is that although we have set no limits to scientific enquiry, it can never furnish us with a complete account of what it is to be a human being or why a human being acts as he does. It will still be reasonable to investigate the working of the body and, in particular, the brain, and to produce mechanical models of the mind. Only, no mechanical model will be completely adequate, nor any explanation in purely physical terms. Models and explanations will continue to be illuminating; but, however

[1] See above, Section 20, pp. 112–113.
[2] See above, Section 10, pp. 47–50.

far they go, there will always remain more to be said. There is no arbitrary bound to scientific enquiry: but no scientific enquiry can ever exhaust the infinite variety of the human mind.

The principle of Universal Causation or the Uniformity of Nature has been differently understood by different thinkers.[1] To some it is simply a methodological principle:[2] Always look for scientific explanations, and if you do not find one, do not give up; assume that you have not found it rather than that it does not exist. To others, perhaps less sophisticated, it is an insight into ontology. It is a truth about Reality. It tells us the way that things are. In the form of the principle of spatio-temporal continuity, it tells us that there are no gaps, no discontinuities in Nature; everything is causally connected, there is no room for any further factor to intervene in the course of events, and there is nothing new under the sun. The methodological form of the principle easily admits of the grace of humility. It is possible, and in certain circumstances for certain purposes reasonable, to pursue a policy of not admitting failure, while acknowledging that one will never be able to claim complete success. Even if I know I shall not be able to find a scientific explanation of every event, I do not know that I shall not be able to find one of *this* event, and therefore it is reasonable to go on looking, since to abandon the search is to resign myself to failure, while to continue is not necessarily fruitless. In the context, therefore, of scientific enquiry, where the only object is to find scientific explanations, and there are no countervailing considerations of cost or of anything else, it is reasonable to adopt, as a methodological principle, that Every event has a cause, that is to say, a scientific explanation. We can adopt it in one context without being thereby obliged to adopt it in all. On Mondays the neurophysiologist, who is, on Sundays, a Methodist lay-preacher, can make the assumption that there are physical causes for every mental event, without thereby being precluded from making a different assumption on Sundays, when he talks of sin and salvation, and preaches and

---

[1] See above, Section 11, pp. 52–55, 60–61.

[2] Kant, *Critique of Pure Reason*, A498/B526; see also, G. J. Warnock, "Every Event has a Cause", in *Logic and Language*, 2nd series, ed. A. G. N. Flew, Oxford, 1953, pp. 95–111. Jonathan Bennett, "The Status of Determinism", *British Journal for the Philosophy of Science*, XIV, 1963–4, pp. 106–119.

prays. He makes his methodological assumption on Mondays, not because it is true but because this is the right assumption for the purpose of his enquiry; just as the solicitor makes the assumption, in drafting a partnership agreement, that all his client's colleagues are untrustworthy and dishonourable, not because in fact they are, but because it is his business to guard against the possibility that they might be. In each case, the assumption is only methodological, and different methods require different assumptions, without any of them being necessarily absolute. Kant's two stand-points become tenable again. We no longer pretend that there is no incompatibility between them. But we deny the all-sufficiency of the scientific stand-point, which had been encroaching on that of moral judgement. The scientific stand-point offers only a limited view of the world for limited purposes. It is optional, not absolute. We assume, *for* the purposes of doing science, *when* we are doing science, *if* we want to do science, that every event has a scientific explanation, just as when we are doing economics we assume the existence of economic man, who buys in the cheapest market and sells in the dearest, and is always out to maximise his profits. But we need not believe that every event really does have a complete scientific explanation, any more than we need believe that men really are embodiments of economic man. It is a useful assumption, no more and no less, but only within limits, and only useful, not true.

The principle of Universal Causation, taken merely as a methodological principle, poses no problems. Perhaps this is how Kant intended his two stand-points to be understood. But most people have found it difficult to avoid reifying their principles, and have therefore been inclined to view the principle of Universal Causation as an insight into ontology, a statement about the nature of things. It is partly that we want to know what Reality is like. We have a natural ontological urge which leads us to interpret policies as truths, and recommendations about method as statements about fact. It is partly, also, that even if we try to stick to the methodological interpretation, we yearn for an architectonic method. It is not enough to have a variety of methodological principles, a variety of stand-points, all optional, all equally valid in their own way. We want to know how they are related, and want to integrate them into one all-embracing, if not very precise, system. The Methodist neurophysiologist cannot keep his principles in two pockets, so that Sunday's morality does not ever come into contact with Monday's medicine. Often, even on week-days, he is having to take moral decisions— whether to perform a pre-frontal leucotomy on a particular patient: always on Sundays he has to take into account the fact that men are not always free, not completely responsible for all their actions. Morality and religion at least cannot take a partial view: they must take everything into account. Therefore their stand-point is not on a par with the limited one of natural science. But if any method is architectonic, then we shall regard it as ontological too, and say that it corresponds to the nature of things. For to say that a thing is real *is* to ascribe to it a privileged status in our scheme of thought, and the most important matters cannot but be regarded as being real. We cannot avoid fundamental philosophical issues by interpreting our principles entirely methodologically. We are bound to be guided, explicitly or implicitly, by ontological considerations too. We are all, here, metaphysicians, though often only covertly. We need to articulate our metaphysical beliefs and bring them into the open, so that we can acknowledge and criticize them, and, if necessary, amend them. Better this than to be swayed by unrecognised metaphysical predilections which we deny, on principle, that we could possibly have.

The great attraction of the principle of Universal Causation is the simple and complete and continuous view of nature that it offers. This is why, all methodological considerations apart, we feel it must be true. It is the best possible God's eye view of the created universe. If we had been making the world, it is just how we should have done the job. So we feel. And if we are to compromise the absolutism of the principle of Universal Causation, we must consider afresh how we shall have to picture the universe. We shall not be able to give a complete account in terms of *things*. Any account in terms of point-particles or other thing-like entities, which when determined for one time are determined for all, will have to include some causal singularities, some cluster-points, some points of infinity, or something else to indicate times and places where causal completeness or causal continuity breaks down. Any account which seeks to avoid inexplicabilities and causal discontinuities must expand its types of explanation and types of cause to include not only regularity explanations but rational ones and not only things but persons, or at least minds.

Rationality is a fundamental category of our thought. It cannot be reduced to regularity alone. Any account of thinking or logic cannot be entirely formal, but must depend on our knowing what it is to be reasonable.[1] We cannot reduce reason to rules, or mind to matter. And therefore we cannot take a completely materialist or determinist view of the universe, but must take Rationality as the fundamental principle. We cannot, so far as our present argument goes, take the further step, and say that Rationality is embodied in persons, although we believe it to be true. But if there are persons, we have to view them in part as rational agents and not entirely as regular-performing things. And if we wish to explain their actions we cannot do so in terms of causal antecedents alone, but must also give reasons, their reasons, for acting as they did.

Their reasons. The reasons have to be theirs, the ones they thought decisive, they chose to act upon. We cannot eliminate the third personal pronoun. We cannot give a complete explanation in terms of impersonal reasons, valid for all men alike. For then we shall have denied freedom, and explained the action without regard to the agent. There remains a tension between the programme of complete explicability and the requirements of freedom. If men have free will, then no complete explanation of their actions can be given, except by reference to themselves. We can give their reasons. But we cannot explain why their reasons were reasons for them. Often there were other reasons, almost if not quite as cogent, for some other course of action. Often we do, and always we can, choose to disregard the weight of reason, and decide upon some other action than that which is reasonable and right. This, the fundamental fact of freedom, seems mysterious. Two people, from the same background, in the same situation, with the same arguments presented to them, decide differently. We ask 'Why?'. No answer can be given, except that the one decided to, and the other not to. This is the point where there has to be an end of answering. Every scheme of explanation, we saw,[2] has some questions it cannot answer. The physical deter-

---

[1] See J. R. Lucas, "The Philosophy of the Reasonable Man", *Philosophical Quarterly*, **13**, 1963, pp. 98–106.

[2] In Section 11, pp. 60–61; Section 20, p. 103.

minist cannot explain why the universe had the configuration he says it must have had at the beginning of time; and similarly the libertarian can be asked, but cannot answer, the question why free agents chose to act in a rational fashion, and not in some other way. Such questions cannot be answered. Asked why I acted, I give my reasons: asked why I chose to accept them as reasons, I can only say 'I just did'. I am answerable for my actions. I am free to choose what I shall do. But I, and only I, am responsible for my choice. The buck stops here.

In discourse more sweet
(For eloquence the soul, song charms the sense)
Others apart sat on a hill retir'd,
In thoughts more elevate, and reason'd high
Of providence, foreknowledge, will, and fate,
Fix'd fate, free will, foreknowledge absolute,
And found no end, in wand'ring mazes lost.

J. Milton: Paradise Lost bk ii, 11. 555ff.

BIBLIOGRAPHY
OF THE GÖDELIAN ARGUMENT

1. ANTICIPATIONS OF THE ARGUMENT FROM SELF-REFERENCE.

JOSEPH, H. W. B., *Some Problems in Ethics*, Oxford, 1931, Chapter 1, esp. pp. 14–15.

LEWIS, C. S., *Miracles*, London, 1947, Chapter 3, esp. p. 27.

MABBOTT, J. D., *Introduction to Ethics*, London, 1966, pp. 115–16.

McTAGGART, J. E., *Philosophical Studies*, London, 1934, p. 193.

MALCOLM, NORMAN, "Conceivability of Mechanism", *Philosophical Review*, LXXVIII, 1968, Sections 22–7, pp. 67–71.

MASCALL, E. L., *Christian Theology and Natural Science*, London, 1956, Chapter 6, Section 2, pp. 212–19.

PRICE, H. H., "The Self-Refutation of Naturalism", *Socratic Digest*, IV, 1948, p. 98.

WICK, WARNER, "Truth's Debt to Freedom", *Mind*, LXXXII, 1964, pp. 527 ff.

2. GÖDEL'S THEOREM AND SIMILAR RESULTS.

CHURCH, ALONZO, "A note on the Entscheidungsproblem", *Journal of Symbolic Logic*, 1, 1936, pp. 40–1, and 101–2.

FINDLAY, J., "Goedelian Sentences: a Non-Numerical Approach", *Mind*, LI, 1942, pp. 259–65.

FITZPATRICK, P. J., "To Gödel via Babel", *Mind*, LXXV, 1966, pp. 332–50.

GÖDEL, KURT, "Über formal unentscheidbare Sätze der Principia Mathematica und verwandter Systeme", Part I, *Monatshefte für Mathematik und Physik*, XXXVIII, 1931, pp. 173–98. English translation, Kurt Gödel, *Lectures at Institute of Advanced Study*, Princeton, 1934; and B. Meltzer, Edinburgh, 1962 (but see review in *Journal of Symbolic Logic*, 30, 1965, pp. 357–9).

HANSON, NORWOOD RUSSELL, "The Gödel Theorem: An Informal Exposition", *Notre Dame Journal of Formal Logic*, 2, 1961, pp. 94–110, and p. 228 (but see review by Alonzo Church, *Journal of Symbolic Logic*, 27, 1962, pp. 471–2).

KALMÁR, LÁSZLÓ, "A simple Construction of Undecidable Propositions in Formal Systems", *Methods*, 2, 1950, pp. 227–31.

LACEY, H., and JOSEPH, G., "What the Gödel Formula Says", *Mind*, LXXVII, 1968, pp. 77–83.

NAGEL, ERNEST and NEWMANN, JAMES R., *Gödel's Proof*, New York, 1958, London, 1959.

ROSSER, J. BARKLEY, "Extensions of some theorems of Gödel and Church", *Journal of Symbolic Logic*, 1, 1936, pp. 87–91.

TARSKI, ALFRED, *Logic, Semantics, Metamathematics*, Oxford, 1956.

TURING, A. M., "On Computable Numbers with an Application to the Entscheidungsproblem", *Proceedings of the London Mathematical Society*, Series 2, 42, 1936, pp. 230–65, and 43, 1937, pp. 544–6.

3. APPLICATION OF GÖDEL'S ARGUMENT CANVASSED.

BRONOWSKI, J., *The Identity of Man*, New York, 1965, pp. 78–80.

NAGEL, ERNEST and NEWMAN, JAMES R., *Gödel's Proof*, London, 1959, pp. 100–2.

POPPER, K. R., "Indeterminism in Quantum Physics and Classical Physics", *British Journal for the Philosophy of Science*, I, 1951, pp. 179–88.

ROGERS, HARTLEY, *Theory of Recursive Functions and Effective Computability* (mimeographed), 1957, Volume I, pp. 152 ff.

ROSENBLOOM, PAUL, *Elements of Mathematical Logic*, New York, 1950, pp. 207–8.

TURING, A. M., "Computing Machinery and Intelligence", *Mind*, LIX, 1950, pp. 444–5; reprinted in James R. Newman, ed., *The World of Mathematics*, IV, New York, 1956, p. 2110; and in Alan Ross Anderson, ed., *Minds and Machines*, Englewood Cliffs, 1964, pp. 15–16.

4. GÖDEL'S ARGUMENT APPLIED.

BRONOWSKI, J., "The Logic of Mind", *American Scientist*, 54, 1966, pp. 1–14.

LUCAS, J. R., "Minds, Machines and Gödel", *Philosophy*, XXXVI, 1961, pp. 112–27; reprinted in Kenneth M. Sayre and Frederick J. Crosson, eds., *The Modeling of Mind*, Notre Dame, 1963, pp. 255–71; and in Alan Ross Anderson, ed., *Minds and Machines*, Englewood Cliffs, 1964, pp. 43–59.

5. CRITICISMS AND DISCUSSION.

(*In this section entries are arranged in order of publication, except that Rejoinders immediately follow the articles to which they reply.*)

PUTNAM, HILARY, "Minds and Machines", in Sydney Hook, ed., *Dimensions of Mind*, New York, 1960 and 1961, p. 142 of 1961 edition; reprinted in Alan Ross Anderson, ed., *Minds and Machines*, Englewood Cliffs, 1964, p. 77.

SMART, J. J. C., "Gödel's Theorem, Church's Theorem and Mechanism", *Synthese*, XIII, 1961, pp. 105–10.

WHITELEY, C. H., "Minds, Machines and Gödel: a reply to Mr. Lucas", *Philosophy*, XXXVII, 1962, pp. 61–2.

GEORGE, F. H., "Minds, Machines and Gödel: another reply to Mr. Lucas", *Philosophy*, XXXVII, 1962, pp. 62–3.

CHARI, C. T. K., "Further Comments on Minds, Machines and Gödel", *Philosophy*, XXXVIII, 1963, pp. 175-8.

SAYRE, K. M. and CROSSON, F.J., eds., *Philosophy and Cybernetics*, Notre Dame, 1967, p. 22.

BENACERRAF, PAUL, "God, the Devil, and Gödel", *The Monist*, 51, 1967, pp. 9–32.

LUCAS, J. R., "Satan Stultified", *The Monist*, 52, 1968, pp. 145–58.

GOOD, I. J., "Human and Machine Logic", *British Journal for the Philosophy of Science*, 18, 1967, pp. 144–7.

LUCAS, J. R., "Human and Machine Logic: a rejoinder", *British Journal for the Philosophy of Science*, 19, 1968, pp. 155–6.

SMART, J. J. C., *Between Science and Philosophy*, New York, 1968, pp. 317 ff.

BOOLOS, GEORGE S., Book Review, *Journal of Symbolic Logic*, 33, 1968, pp. 613–15.

WEBB, JUDSON, "Metamathematics and the Philosophy of Mind", *Philosophy of Science*, 35, 1968, pp. 156–78.

LUCAS, J. R., "Metamathematics and the Philosophy of Mind: a rejoinder", *Philosophy of Science*, 38, 1971.

LEWIS, DAVID, "Lucas against Mechanism", *Philosophy*, XLIV 1969, pp. 231–3.

CODER, DAVID, "Goedel's Theorem and Mechanism", *Philosophy*, XLIV, 1969, pp. 234–7.

LUCAS, J. R., "Mechanism: a rejoinder", *Philosophy*, XLV, 1970. pp. 149–151.

TURNER, MERLE B., *Realism and the Explanation of Behaviour*, New York, 1970.

INDEX

All references are to page numbers unless a section is indicated (§).
The most important references are given in bold type.